Bridging the Origins Divide

Bridging the Origins Divide

How We Got Here
(and Why It Matters)

by
Paul Myrant

Table of Contents

Preface   vii

Chapter One
Origins: How We Got Here (and Why It Matters)   1

Chapter Two
Five Arguments for God's Existence   17

Chapter Three
Why It Matters   39

Chapter Four
Faith Versus Science   46

Chapter Five
The Nature of the Creator   60

Chapter Six
Who is the Creator?   75

Chapter Seven
Theodicy: When God Doesn't Answer Prayer   81

Chapter Eight
How Were the Heavens and Earth Created?   101

Chapter Nine
Why a Young Earth Matters   122

Chapter Ten
The Greatest Lie Ever Told 132

Chapter Eleven
Dating the Rocks: Radiometric Dating 150

Appendix One:
Talking Points 164

Appendix Two:
Is the Bible a Myth? 168

Appendix Three:
The Problem of Religion 170

Appendix Four:
Anti-Supernaturalism 172

Appendix Five:
Starlight and Time 174

Preface

Throughout human history, the question of a Creator's existence generally centered around which god and which religion—mine or yours. Then came Darwin, who questioned the need for God or any creator. This opened the door for other scientists and renowned thinkers to celebrate creation without God.

Can we explain the existence of the universe without referring to an all-powerful creator? World-renowned astrophysicists Michio Kaku and Neil deGrasse Tyson believe in a god of order and beauty; at least, they are open to that possibility. Though they reject the God of the Bible, they are open to the God of Einstein. Even renowned atheists have come to recognize the universe as too organized and beautiful to have been created without an intelligence.

This book provides a logical and philosophical response to the questions around God's existence, nature and how He created the heavens and earth. I am not a scientist, nor the son of one. I am a philosopher, apologist and biblical theologian. I have spent much of my life researching and studying the philosophies that drive both science and biblical worldviews. I have examined every viewpoint of Genesis 1-11 and how they interact with the whole of Scripture.

I demonstrate three things: belief in God is the best and most logical conclusion that explains the creation of the heavens and earth and all living things; what the Creator is like; and how the Creator made the universe.

On this third point I am focused on the defense of the Genesis narrative as a valid perspective on Creation. Primarily, this is a discussion between the Young Earth Community (YEC) and the Old Earth Community (OEC). These two groups are generally a part of the Christian community. The OEC believes the earth is 4.5 billion years old, and some believe all life evolves from a single-celled organism. The YEC believes the earth is between 6,000 and 10,000 years old and that God created all life intact and complete.

Anyone who has objectively studied these perspectives will realize both represent valid scientific points of view. Each opinion is based on different assumptions. I don't believe you can categorically prove one perspective over the other. Bias, suppositions and worldviews color the arguments.

I am convinced of the Scripture's authority. The old earth worldview is based on false assumptions leading to what I call "scientism"—absolute conclusions made by members of the scientific community based on unproven and unprovable assumptions.

Uniformity, naturalism, anti-supernaturalism and anti-catastrophism are the basic assumptions to which scientists hold. These assumptions color the interpretation of data we find in geology and cosmology. Conclusions based on these are speculative and should always be stated as such.

In the final analysis, if the Bible is true and Earth is 6,000 years old, then the data "found" by science has been wrongly interpreted. The question is, what can we know for sure?

Chapter One

Origins: How We Got Here
(and Why It Matters)

This book focuses on creationism, evolution and the apparent division between religion and science. We will address two questions that have dogged humanity throughout the ages—how we got here and why it matters. In answering these questions, we will examine three concepts: Is there a creator? If so, what is the creator like? If so, how did the creator make the universe?

Who owns the universe?

Imagine you have been lost deep in a forest or jungle for several days. You stumble into a clearing, and to your great relief and surprise, you find a house. You go to the front door and knock. There is no answer, so you go to the back door. You knock, and again there is no response. You are desperate for food and water, but being a civil person, you do not want to break in. You knock on the windows and call out, hoping someone will hear you and invite you in. All remains quiet. Finally, you decide to go inside. You are surprised to find the front door unlocked, so you enter cautiously. You continue to call out as you search each room. "Hello! Hello! Anybody here?" You find no one. To your relief you discover plenty of food and water in the kitchen. You decide you must use some of the resources to stay alive. By early evening, your exhausted body is ready for sleep, so you choose a bed on which to rest. You sleep deeply and long into the next day.

You are greatly refreshed and relieved at being spared by this good fortune. After days, weeks and months no one shows up, and you become increasingly comfortable. You were desperately lost when you first came upon the house, so you decided to stay. There was plenty of food, water and everything you needed to survive.

You are lonely and miss family and friends, but you are safe and quite content. You begin to examine the house—food supply, refrigerator, plumbing and electricity—trying to figure out how everything works. You admire the construction of the house and the design of the rooms. You may wonder how old it is or how it was built.

Yet, in all your questions, you have forgotten the most important and basic question of all: who owns this house? To whom do these resources belong? Who owns the land, and who bought the materials to build the home? To whom should you be thankful?

We can and should ask the same questions concerning our remarkable Earth. As far as we know, it is the only planet in the universe capable of sustaining life. We are the perfect distance from the sun and have the perfect atmosphere, water and climate to sustain us. Food grows on plants and trees we never planted, and there is an amazing variety of fish and animals to eat.

Could this be an accident? Or is it a message from the Creator? If we find a house in the forest that can sustain us and provide all we need for survival, we know it had a builder and an owner. Since we find ourselves on a planet capable of sustaining and providing all things we need, we know it must have had a builder and an owner.

"Gravity may put the planets into motion, but without the divine Power, it could never put them into such a circulating motion as they have about the Sun; and therefore, for this as well as other reasons, I am compelled to ascribe the frame of this System to an intelligent Agent.[1]

"All variety of created objects which represent order and life in the universe could happen only by the willful reasoning of its original Creator, whom I call the Lord God."[2]

—Sir Isaac Newton

How did we get here?

If you lived in California in 1885 and awoke one morning to find a 1985 DeLorean in your barn, you would rightly ask what it was and how it got there. Without concrete evidence, some might be tempted to believe it magically appeared. One might even consider it to be divine and deserving of worship. Everyone would question what it was and how it got there. Some might undertake an examination to determine its origin and how it works.

Since you are aware of metal, you could deduce aspects of

---

1   www.brainyquote.com/quotes/isaac_newton_737919
2   IBID

how it could have been made, though creating it yourself would be way beyond your skill or expertise. All this would be considered empirical observations.

However, there can be no direct empirical evidence of how it was made and how it got into your garage. Its placement was not and cannot be observed; it is beyond your comprehension. Unless an eyewitness comes forward, you can never know how or why it was put there.

What you can know for certain (albeit axiomatically), is that someone or some being with intelligence and power created the DeLorean and placed it into your barn. No scientist would assume it magically appeared or that it created itself and placed itself into your barn. Logic and reason dictate the DeLorean was made and transported by someone greater and more powerful than the farmer who found it.

Unlike the 1885 discovery and examination of the DeLorean, we find ourselves in an environment we did not create. From our beginning we have asked, "How and why am I here? For millennia, thinkers have pondered this deep and significant question.

For the past 500 years, scientists and philosophers have diligently investigated and theorized about an answer to this conundrum. Many, especially scientists, have abandoned the possibility that we got here through a power greater than ourselves. They are determined to find the answer without considering supernatural or other worldly causes. Instead, they focus on how things work and devise possible theories about how the universe was created (means of creation). They reject or at least ignore the possibility of an intelligent, powerful being behind it all.

Even if we could discover the *means* of creation, it would not tell us *why* the universe and all living things were created. What is the meaning and purpose of living beings? Is there objective morality, absolute right and wrong? To whom do the heavens and earth belong?

Science, Religion, Philosophy

The existence of God is a philosophical question and has nothing to do with science or religion. The differences between science and philosophy, and philosophy and religion, are often misunderstood.

Many scientists believe God's existence is a scientific question to which science will provide the final answer. However, science can neither prove nor disprove God's existence. They may discover how the universe was created but can never prove the who or why of creation.

Conversely, many spiritual leaders and individuals believe the existence of God is a religious question based in part on their personal faith. There are many philosophical arguments used to support faith in a creator. These arguments are not inherently religious, and they do not prove God exists any more than scientific arguments.

The Bible never seeks to prove there is a God; rather, it declares God exists and is the cause for the heavens, the earth and all living things.

Belief in a creator is a philosophical question that can only be answered by appealing to reason and simple logic. There are only two options: the heavens and earth were created, or they created themselves. They were either caused or uncaused. They either magically appeared out of nothing, or they were brought into existence by a being capable of doing so.

—Sir Isaac Newton

Whether God exists is the first of several questions that center around this topic. How did matter come to be? How was matter structured and designed? How did living things come into existence? Does life have meaning? Is there objective morality? Is there a soul? Is there any purpose to life? To say no to God's existence is to leave all these questions without an answer. All things end up being random and subjective without any meaning or purpose behind them.

Dr. Michio Kaku, co-inventor of string theory, recently admitted that science could not prove or disprove the existence of God. He stated:

"Science is based on what is testable, reproducible and falsifiable. That's called science. However, there are certain things that are not testable, not reproducible and not falsifiable. And that would include the existence of God."[4]

Scientists do have an opinion on the existence of a creator. In fact, all beliefs about a creator's existence are mere opinions. We must make a distinction between the means of creation (the how, or the process used to bring matter, energy, light and life into existence) and the underlying cause.

Do we live in a caused or uncaused universe? Can material things be their own cause? Can matter or its preatomic elements create themselves? If the Big Bang caused the universe to come into existence, what caused the elements and underlying

---

3   Isaac Newton www.brainyquote.com/quotes/isaac_newton_737919
4   (bigthink.com/culture-religion/

                                              Bridging the Origins Divide

functionality to exist? How did gravity, electromagnetism, the strong and weak nuclear forces come into existence? To answer these questions, we must engage in a rational conversation based on logic and reason.

The best and most rational response to the existence of the universe is that it was caused. Logically, inanimate objects existing and functioning without a cause are highly improbable, if not impossible. Non-living, highly structured atoms and molecules require an intelligent being behind their existence. Adding to that difficulty, atoms and molecules exist in innumerable quantities, identical to all others in their category. For example, gold atoms have 79 protons all identical to one another. How could so many identical atoms exist? Their numbers are incalculable. There are millions of living organisms that also require a cause outside themselves, a being or intelligence greater than themselves.

Conversely, belief in a creator does not necessarily make a person religious. Proposing a creator as the cause of creation is simply a philosophical explanation for the existence of the heavens, the earth and all living things. Belief in a creator is a rational explanation for our existence. Some scientists say there is no evidence for a creator; however, creation itself is evidence—just as the computers, keyboards and monitors we use are evidence that there is someone who makes computers.

Religion is a set of beliefs and practices based on what different people and groups believe about a creator and how that creator expects them to behave. Being religious does not mean you are anti-science, anti-reason or a member of a cult. Neither does it make you righteous or a good person. It does not mean you are right about your beliefs, political ideologies or behavior.

Nor does it mean you have a relationship with the creator and are representing him when you speak.

While science cannot prove or disprove the existence of a creator, theories abound concerning how the universe was created. Understanding the means of creation is a secondary question to the creator's existence. We must first decide if there *is* a creator—a being who is the cause for the universe and all living things. Answering this question will tell us many things about the nature of the creator, including possible ways the universe and all living things were made.

Without appealing to a creator, what is the basis for meaning, morality and human existence? Can there be objective morality and meaning, or do individual leaders of society determine right and wrong? Is morality based on whomever is in power or the most persuasive person in the room? These issues are on par with asking where matter comes from. Of course, we still need to answer where the creator himself came from.

The Darwin Effect

Throughout history, few have questioned the existence of God. Most arguments were about which God—mine or yours. Since the enlightenment, the question has gradually turned toward the existence of and nature of God. In the Western world the Scriptures have been a primary source of information and education since Constantine. Religions (Judaism, Islam and Christianity) have been engaged in an ongoing conflict as to which faith was "true." Numerous wars and horrific acts have occurred between Islam and Judaism, Christianity and Islam, and shamefully within various sects of the Christian faith.

The Age of Enlightenment brought forth intellectualism. Professional educators and scientists have changed the narrative from faith to reason. They rejected the supernatural and focused primarily on naturalism and empirical evidence. The idea of God's existence began to cast serious doubt within the intellectual minds of the world. Most of these leaders were not outright atheists but sought to see the world apart from the Bible and religion.

For several centuries, scientists such as Baruch Spinoza (a forerunner to the age of enlightenment) have questioned the Scriptures' perspective on God. Higher critics challenged the authorship of the Torah. They questioned the accuracy of the dates they were written, and the role Moses played in its transmission. Numerous men participated in this attack on the Scriptures. Their common belief was a rejection of the supernatural world and the Bible, which was considered a magical book ostensibly given to us by God.

A growing disbelief among these "scholars" gave rise to Hutton, Lyell, Darwin and Wellhausen, whose works laid the foundation for the greatest lie ever told. These most influential skeptics were about to undermine reason, faith and morality like none before them.

Hutton, Lyell, Darwin and Wellhausen
These four skeptics transformed a nominal Christian world into a secular, wanna-be, anti-Christian utopia. James Hutton and Charles Lyell developed the theory of uniformity, which claims that the geology of the earth is the result of millions of years of erosion and uplift along with other natural processes.

Uniformity's long geological ages opened the door for the theory of evolution. Uniformity provided the theoretical time Darwin needed for evolution to take place. Both philosophies directly contradict a literal six-day creation—the simplest interpretation of the biblical record.

Following on the heels of Darwin, higher criticism took the lead. Higher criticism is a school of thought that questions the authorship, dating and accuracy of the biblical texts. Specifically, this challenge focused on the first five books of the Bible.

Theologians who had already rejected the authority of the Bible began to publicly question the historical accuracy of the recorded events. Julius Wellhausen popularized the Documentary Hypothesis *(See Appendix 2)* along with a variety of similar theories which espouse an anti-supernatural view of the Scriptures. Wellhausen was directly influenced by naturalism, uniformity and the advent of Darwin's theory of evolution.

As this new theology and scientific worldview took hold in Western civilization, evolution's primary philosophy of naturalism replaced a supernatural view of the world and creation. Naturalism replaced faith in God, the biblical record, miracles and belief in a supernatural realm.

In many mainline Christian churches, belief in the Bible digressed from being the very words of God and a reliable source of historical truth to a collection of fables, myths and abstract religious beliefs.

Archeology and conservative Christian scholarship have repeatedly demonstrated the historical accuracy of the scriptures. However, many congregations, denominations, colleges and seminaries were unable to undo the progressive erosion of biblical authority.

In Europe, these challenges to biblical authority have had a devastating effect on historic Christianity. The 21st century church is only a shell of its former self. In his book, *The Suicide of the West*, James Burnham eloquently states, "The West remembers enough about Christianity to feel guilty for its

Bridging the Origins Divide

sins but not enough to recall where forgiveness comes from."[5]

The effect in America, while significant, was not as widespread. Fundamentalist religious groups in the United States successfully responded to and rebuffed these attacks. Americans are surprisingly strong in their belief in a personal creator, the rejection of evolution, and acceptance of the Genesis account of creation.

> *Fifty-three percent of adults believe God created human beings in their present form exactly the way the Bible describes it. Thirty-one percent believe humans evolved over millions of years from other forms of life with God having guided the process, and 12 percent said humans have evolved over millions of years from other forms of life without intervention from God.[6]*

By comparison,

> *"Only 7 percent of those surveyed in Great Britain said they take the biblical creation account of Genesis 1 literally [...] Respondents in Germany, Norway, Russia and the Netherlands all ranked significantly lower than the United States in biblical literalism."[7]*

More recent surveys show the number of Americans who believe in a creator and the biblical record remains high, but there is a fast-growing component moving to a non-religious status.

> *Forty percent of US adults subscribe to a strict creationist view of human origins, believing that God created them*

---

5   Burnham, James. "Suicide of the West". The John Day Company, New York, NY. USA
6   news.gallup.com/poll/647594/
7   www.secularhumanism.org/library

in their present form within roughly the past 10,000 years. However, more Americans continue to think that humans evolved over millions of years—either with God's guidance (33%) or without God's involvement at all (22%).

As many as 47% and as few as 38% of Americans have taken a creationist view of human origins throughout Gallup's 37-year trend. Likewise, between 31% and 40% of US adults have attributed humans' development to a combination of evolution and divine intervention over the same period.[8]

There have been dramatic changes in Western Europe since the first edition of this book. Recently, *Creationism in Europe* was published by Johns Hopkins University Press.

It is based on five years of research, during which the team trawled through newspaper articles, internet sites, scientific studies, opinion polls, and reports by scientists in other European countries. Creationism, the belief that a god—not evolution—shaped life on Earth, is by no means restricted to people from the Bible belt in the US or illiterates in remote corners of civilization.

In fact, it's spreading in the very stronghold of evolution, Europe. That's the conclusion of five years of research that's been put into a new book on creationism. The book details how creationism is on the march throughout most of Europe.

"Creationism is most dominant in Eastern Europe and Turkey, but even some schools in the Netherlands are

---

8   news.gallup.com/poll/261680/

                                    Bridging the Origins Divide

teaching creationism," says one of the book's authors Hans Henrik Hjermitslev, University College South Denmark. "Politicians in some German federal states are advocating that schools use creationist books alongside those about evolutionary theory in their lessons. This kind of struggle is going on, on a small scale in many places."[9]

Across Western Europe, most people say they believe in God. But in today's culture, believing in God does not necessarily mean belief in the God of the Bible.

Indeed, even though all 15 countries surveyed are histor-ically Christian, and nearly all of them still have Chris-tian majorities, fewer respondents say they believe in God "as described in the Bible" than say they believe in "some other higher power or spiritual force." And sub-stantial numbers of people surveyed across the region do not believe there is any higher power or spiritual force in the universe.

Belief in the biblical God is much more common among church-attending Christians than it is among non-prac-ticing Christians (those who attend church no more than a few times a year). While most non-practicing Chris-tians say they do believe in God or some other higher power, most say they do not believe in God as described in the Bible. And among religiously unaffiliated people in Western Europe, the prevailing view is that there is no higher power of any kind.[10]

While there is encouraging news in these statistics, we know

---

9   sciencenordic.com/creationism
10   ibid

that those affiliated with non-religious beliefs are the fastest growing segment of society.

In America, progressive Christianity has made large inroads in traditionally conservative congregations—abandoning a literal reading of Genesis 1 and 2; adopting female pastors, bishops and elders; and an openness to aspects of the LGBTQ community. All these compromises began with a rejection of a literal understanding of Genesis 1 and 2.

The "Facts" of Evolution

Evolution is still taught as fact throughout the West's public-school systems. From elementary school through college, evolution is drilled into the minds and hearts of young people. *National Geographic* and *The Discovery Channel* continually tell us the earth is billions of years old. *The History Channel* speaks almost exclusively from an anti-supernatural view of the Bible; it continually questions biblical history and authority.

The long-term effect of these philosophies and the demise of authority of the Scriptures has led, in part, to the moral relativism that shapes contemporary Western cultures. Absolute right and wrong have vanished from the hearts and minds of many; people believe and do that which is right in their own eyes. *"If a creator exists, he is absent and unconcerned."* Beliefs which consider absolute laws of God have given way to beliefs based on feelings and stories of individuals who live on the fringe of society.

This challenge to Christianity is enormous. It has been marginalized and excluded from significant conversations taking place in our communities. In general, Christianity and religion have no say in the important topics we face. In the spirit of broadening the discourse, a foundation for the existence

Bridging the Origins Divide

of a caring God who is recognized as a personal being and is involved in our lives must be discussed in our communities. The Bible teaches that God's existence is an innate truth written on the soul of every person.

> *"The fear of the Lord is the beginning of wisdom."*
>
> —Proverbs 1:7 NIV, Solomon

> *"He that comes to God must believe that he is and that he rewards those who diligently seek him."*
>
> —Hebrews 11:6 NIV

> *"…That which is known about God is evident within them, for God made it evident to them. For since the creation of the world His invisible attributes, His eternal power and divine nature have been clearly seen, being understood through what has been made."*
>
> —Romans 1:19, 20. NASB, The Apostle Paul.

The Psalmist David Wrote,

> *The heavens declare the glory of God; the skies proclaim the works of His hands. Day after day they pour forth speech; night after night they display knowledge. There is no speech or language where their voice is not heard. Their voice goes out into all the earth, their words to the end of the world.*
>
> —Psalm 19:1-4 NIV

Belief in a creator is the foundation of all rational thought. Apart from this foundation, humankind is left without a compass to navigate the myriads of personal philosophies espoused by humanity. However, if Paul's statements are true, we should be able to examine the universe and through the process of deduction and reason demonstrate the existence and nature of the creator. This will in turn provide us with an objective source for belief in God apart from the aid of religion.

Chapter Two

Five Arguments for God's Existence

The existence of God has been discussed by great religious leaders, philosophers and scientists since the beginning of time. A modern and common belief is that science will prove or disprove this. Creation scientists, pastors and religious leaders are generally considered ignorant buffoons by the mainstream scientific community, and their opinions are largely ignored.

Michio Kaku, an American theoretical physicist and futurist, has stated,

"I have concluded that we are in a world made by rules created by an intelligence. To me, it is clear that we exist in a plan which is governed by rules that were created, shaped by a universal intelligence and not by chance."[11]

Argument One: Matter Exists

In 1965, The Lovin' Spoonful band recorded the famous pop tune, *Do You Believe in Magic,* which peaked at number 9 on the Billboard Hot 100 chart. This could be a theme song for atheistic evolution. Magic is the only explanation science has for the existence of the universe and all living things.

Something has always existed. Imagine there is nothing—no people, animals or any living thing; no sun, moon, stars, planets or space itself; none of the four elementary forces of nature and no creator. There could be only one conclusion: the universe and all living things accidentally appeared out of nowhere with no cause, without reason and with no assistance from an intelligent being. In other words, it magically appeared—hardly a scientific response.

Logic dictates that someone or something is eternal; there is no other option. Three possibilities exist: The Creator is eternal, matter is eternal, or pre-atomic material is eternal. However, if matter is eternal how did it get here, and how was it shaped into objects and the living things we see? If pre-atomic material had always existed, where did it come from and how did things become what they are? Skeptic David Hume (1722–1776) once remarked on the supposed need for a creator and asked,

> *"Why may not the material universe be the necessarily existent Being? There is no warrant [reason] for going beyond the universe to posit a supernatural ground of its existence."[12]*

Hume was making the argument that matter is eternal and that the universe is its own cause. However, if the Big Bang is the cause for the universe (which most scientists believe it is), it would mean the universe did not exist at a point in the past to even come into existence. This means it had to be created by

---

12 David Hume, Dialogues concerning Natural Religion, ed (Indianapolis: Bobbs-Merrill, 1947), pt. IX, p. 190.

Bridging the Origins Divide

someone or something. Whoever or whatever caused it is the creator of all things. Dr. Stephen Hawking agrees. He said,

> *"So long as the universe had a beginning, we could suppose it had a Creator."[13]*

Thus, what the Big Bang model requires is that the universe began to exist and was created out of nothing. Scientist Victor Stenger speaks about scientists who believe in God. He calls them "Premise Keepers":

> *"To the Premise-Keeper, the big bang provides "evidence" that creation took place in time … Something cannot come from nothing, and so the universe needs a Creator. That the Creator must have come from nothing is finessed away. God is a different "logical type" than the universe—a type that does not require creation. Theologians do not make clear why the universe itself cannot be of this logical type."[14]*

Stenger clearly understands the issue. He seems to agree that something always had to exist. However, instead of a creator being the cause for the universe, he believes the universe is eternal and created itself. Here's my perspective:

> *"The reason the universe cannot be its own cause, is because matter is inert, it has no will, intellect, or capacity to bring itself into existence, and then shape itself into all the variety of matter that exists, especially in the mass quantity and incredible variety of living things. If you want to say that matter itself is the living apparatus,*

---

13 Stephen Hawking, A Brief History of Time (New York: Bantam, 1988), p. 140-41
    Stephen Hawking,
14 Stenger, Victor. www.secularhumanism.org/library/fi/stenger_19_1.html

the intelligent power, with forethought, and the ability to shape shift itself into itself, be my guest. This belief system is not scientific, it is like claiming the computer I am typing on created itself. It is a form of pantheism, a religious belief that claims, "everything is god".

In either case, the premise is sound. For matter and life to exist today, something or someone always had to exist. Theoretically, it could be the universe; however, we will show that a creator is the more logical option.

Is it possible for matter to be its own cause?

Matter is not magical. Atoms, molecules, light, energy and innumerable particles are real. The creation of matter requires intelligence, will and ability. Matter would have to be intelligent and capable of causing itself to come into existence. It would be capable of shaping and designing itself, planning and executing its own creation. Matter would need to be powerful enough to stretch the universe into existence and somehow create life.

Matter consists of non-living entities that were shaped and formed by something other than themselves. The amount of matter in the universe is incalculable. The sheer volume of matter could only have been caused by someone or something greater than that which exists.

Could preatomic material be the eternal cause of all things?

This is impossible for the same reasons. An explanation is required for how matter or preatomic material got here and how it could have been shaped and formed into inert and living things. To reject the concept of a creator as the cause for all things is to believe in magic. The universe and all living things

Bridging the Origins Divide

would have suddenly appeared on their own without intervention from an intelligent being.

There must be a creator.

Logically, we must conclude that a creator planned, shaped, designed and caused all things to come into existence. But from where did the creator come. Since something always existed, the creator must be eternal. It may be difficult to comprehend, but it is the best possible explanation for our existence.

Argument Two: Matter Is Shaped and Designed

Shapes are an integral part of objects and living things. They are critical aspects of design. The sun, moon and stars are all spheres. Plants, animals and human beings have distinct shapes.

Generally, shape is intentional as it is with the sun, moon and stars. However, the shape of a bird is more critical to its design and purpose than the shape of a rock. Rocks and mountains are shaped, but they are blobs of undefined matter. Rocks and mountains are randomly scattered about the earth and universe.

Randomness can be intentional or accidental. Modern artists intentionally splatter paint on a canvas for effect. It is random because it is not measured or specific; it is intentional because the process is premeditated.

If a paint shaker machine loses its grip on a can of paint which then splatters around the hardware store, it is accidental randomness. The resultant splatter shapes, though random, are accidental. Due to infinitely possible shapes, it would be conceivable to eventually discover a shape that resembles the Virgin Mary, Carl Sagan or even the United States. However, it would be an unintentionally random event.

The initial creation of the earth involved artistry and design—hills and valleys, beaches and plains. Dirt and stone and all the elements on and in the earth have beauty and value. All these were made and shaped intentionally, and served multiple purposes. Cosmetically, they are beautiful to behold and provide great enjoyment for humanity.

However, the mountains and geology of today's earth are not random; it was part of the process that shaped the earth after the global flood. The process would be predictable considering the forces engaged in the destruction of the first earth, massive amounts of rain, earthquakes and vulcanism around the globe.

While the simple existence of matter demands a creator, the nature of matter demands an intelligent, powerful and capable creator. Atoms and molecules have a specific structure—a nucleus and various numbers of protons, neutrons and electrons. Molecules are composed of two or more atoms. They are unique and specifically structured.

On a molecular level everything in the universe has a unique shape and structure, and they are distinct from one another. They are designed to be what they are.

Matter is intricately designed and engineered for a specific purpose. That purpose may be unknown, but it relates directly to the external shapes and internal designs.

Richard Dawkins detailed the intelligence of bats and their possible evolutionary beginnings. He proposed how an engineer might solve the problem of how they could be capable of navigating in the dark. He imagines what it must have been like for animals that had to learn survival. On their own and without capability, they created and transformed themselves into functional creatures. Bats developed biological active sonar (echolocation) so they could fly and hunt at night. "If you saw an object shaped like a bat on the ground, most people would recognize what it was. If you examined the bat closely and discovered that it was a rubber toy, you would realize that there is much more to a bat's design than just its shape. The inner structure of the bat is equally as important as its outer shape. It must have muscles and bones that support its weight. Without a small brain that allows it to fly and a sonar system, it would walk around on its legs and probably be eaten or die of starvation. The bat's highly developed sonar system allows it to fly in the dark night, and in caves, without running into walls or other objects"

> *"Dawkins attributes the nocturnal activity of the bat to his belief that there were too many animals already hunting in the daytime. There was not enough food for the bats, so they decided to fly at night when it was less populated. Of course, they had a problem with how to fly at night, so bats decided to develop sonar so they could fly at night and then proceeded to do so."[15]*

Self-designing bats are improbable. They do not have the power or will to make these choices or the ability to change themselves. They must have been created with qualities we see today. The structural design of all things is proof that an intelligent, capable being created, shaped and designed matter.

This proposal is symptomatic of the difficulty in explaining an uncaused, purposeless, universe creating itself. Dawkins,

---

15 Dawkins, Richard. The Blind Watchmaker WW Norton & Company, New York, London, 1987, 22,23. Quoted from Myrant, Paul, The Challenge of Evolution: 2009 Tate Publishing, pg. 56

through reason and logical cognition, attempted to explain the existence of complex living entities without the aid of a creator. He is himself a component of a shaped and designed universe living in denial of reality.

Argument Three: Shape and Design=Meaning and Purpose
Everything is shaped, designed and created for a purpose. Some things are primarily cosmetic such as a sunrise or sunset. They are beautiful and inspiring to behold but do little else for us.

The sun (our star) is also designed. Its heat prevents the earth from becoming a deep freeze and destroying everything on the planet. The sun's rays provide vitamin D which keeps us healthy and functioning.

Stars are often used for navigational purposes by sailors, but for the most part they are cosmetic. Other than our sun, stars give us no light to read by and no heat to warm us, but who does not stare in wonder at the night sky full of these great balls of fire? Who is not amazed at the sight of the birth or death of a star as seen through the eye of the Hubble or Webb telescope?

A sunset can instill hope, encouragement and refreshment. When we view a photograph or painting of a sunset, we appreciate the painter or photographer. How often do we ignore the creator and the sunsets he has given us day after day from the beginning of time?

Every invention built by human hands was designed with a purpose. It is illogical to believe all the amazing, highly structured things on earth could exist without the specific involvement of human creators.

Vacuum cleaners are ugly and odd-looking, but they are shaped and designed for a very specific purpose. No rational human being would suggest that they shaped, designed and

Bridging the Origins Divide

created themselves. Yet this is exactly what atheistic science is telling you about the heavens and the earth. Out of nothing everything came into being on its own for no specific reason. It is purpose without meaning.

> *"The total number of tree species on Earth is around 73,000, including roughly 9,000 not yet known to science."[16]*

Each tree is shaped, designed, distinct from other trees, and can reproduce innumerable times.

> *"The grass family includes over 11,500 accepted species, some grass taxonomists (Agrostologists) estimate there are as many as 13,000 species, considering their taxonomy is still a work in progress."[17]*

Each blade of grass is shaped, designed and distinct from other blades of grass and can reproduce innumerable times.

Life forms:

> *"Estimates range from 3 million to 100 million or even more. Taxonomists—biologists who specialize in identifying and classifying life on the planet—have named approximately 1.7 million species so far. Each year, in contrast, the lion's share of unknown species are small, mostly microscopic organisms that live in some of Earth's least-accessible habitats: beneath the ground, in the deep sea, in the crowns of tropical trees, and on the backs or in the guts of other creatures. Such insects, worms, mites, fungi, bacteria and other tiny life forms are what Harvard University biologist Edward O. Wilson calls "the*

---

16 seas.umich.edu/globalchangebiology/
17 naturalhistory.si.edu/research/botany/research/grass-research

black hole of taxonomy." Unimaginably abundant, their numbers could alter overall species totals by a factor of 10 or more."[18]

Design and purpose are opposite sides of the same coin. Design focuses on shape and appeal, while purpose reveals how an object is used and how it works. Purpose is *why* something was designed. Purpose gives objects and living things meaning, and meaning gives them value. Everything has purpose and value even if unknown to us.

Argument Four: Mankind

How were living things created and what brought life into existence? The creation of life is vastly more complex and complicated than simple matter. Neither could happen without a creator.

In answering the question, "Where does life come from?"[19] Dawkins ironically asks for a small miracle. He is implying there is at least a small degree of randomness necessary for the existence of life. Let's assume that Dawkins gets his miracle of life.[20] Is it more likely this small spark of life would have died or survived? Under what circumstances is it conceivable that this accidental, extremely fragile, spark of life survives?

Unless life entered the world in a mature form and capable of survival in a hostile environment, it is not reasonable to believe it would survive. Perhaps if life was created in perfect laboratory conditions, it might have a chance to survive. However, evolution's "spark of life" would have been very fragile, and survival would not have been assured.

Even in safe environments, newborn infants and animals

---

18 www.nwf.org/Magazines/National-Wildlife/1999
19 Dawkins, Richard. The Blind Watchmaker WW Norton & Company, New York, London, 1987
20 IBID

                                  Bridging the Origins Divide

require a great deal of care to survive. Without a designer and creator, it is difficult to believe that life could begin or survive under less safe conditions. Evolution's "spark of life" would have had to occur many times, perhaps many hundreds or thousands of times. What are the chances of a second miracle happening, or even a third and fourth? How many miracles are required for life not only to exist, but to survive and thrive?

Lighting a fire in the wilderness by rubbing two sticks together is a difficult task. It requires skill, the right implements, great energy and perseverance to start a flame. Once you have started the fire, it must be constantly nurtured, or it will be quickly extinguished.

It requires a tremendous amount of blind faith to believe that life came into existence on its own and for no reason, then to survive without aid in a hostile environment. It's even more difficult to believe when you realize all life forms live a relatively short time. Author Thomas Hayden, in the July 2002 *US News and World Report*, writes:

> *"Scientists have learned that our planet has been rocked periodically by catastrophes: enormous volcanic eruptions that belched carbon dioxide, creating a super greenhouse effect; severe cold spells that left much of the planet enveloped in ice; collisions with asteroids. These convulsions killed off much of life's diversity."*[21]

With these massive catastrophes, shouldn't the evolutionary process begin time and time again? Hopefully, the more evolved flatworm survived the meteor strike. If the un-evolved flatworm survived instead, would it have to go through the entire evolutionary cycle again? In the same article, Hayden says,

---

21   Hayden, Thomas. A Theory Evolves. US News and World Report, July 29, 2002.

"'Half an eye would be worse than none,' creationists were fond of arguing. But partial eyes turn out to be common in nature, and biologists can trace eye evolution from the lensless flatworm eyespot to the complex geometry of vertebrate eyes."[22]

Biologists cannot trace this process; they hypothesize about it. There is no conclusive proof or direct evidence of an eye in biological transition. All eyes are attached to completely formed living creatures. Should every creature have a "complete" eye? The *lensless* flatworm seems to have what it needs to function and survive.

Imagine an "evolution" of Adam and Eve. It would be impossible for Adam to have evolved from a single-classed entity; however, that is only half the problem. Both Adam and Eve would have had to evolve separately and simultaneously in a perfectly sustainable environment in which heat, water, shelter, food and everything else was present. We could just as likely have had Adam and Evan rather than Adam and Eve.

Can random chance produce life?

Random chance cannot account for the complex design of DNA. It is statistically and mathematically impossible. Harold Morowitz once calculated that the chances of a free-living, single-celled organism such as a bacterium might form by combining preexistent building blocks would be about 1:100,000,000,000.[23] Sir Fred Hoyle calculated that the chances of simple proteins forming an amoeba were $1:10^{40,000}$. The odds calculated by Morowitz and Hoyle are staggering.

The chances of winning a state lottery every week from the age of 18 to 99 are better than the odds of a single-celled organ-

---

22   IBID
23   www.khouse.org/enews_article/2006/1082/accessed January 18, 2008

          Bridging the Origins Divide

ism being formed by random chance. The probability of spontaneous generation is about the same as the probability that a tornado sweeping through a junkyard could assemble a 747 from the contents therein.[24]

Dawkins agrees with this conclusion. He said,

"We have seen that living things are too improbable and too beautifully designed to have come into existence by chance. Furthermore, the amount of information in a fertilized human egg is astounding and could not be the result of a random process."[25]

Although scientists have learned a great deal about the human genome, the overwhelming majority of DNA remains a complete mystery. According to Dr. Jerry Bergman, professor of science at Northwest College,

"At the moment of conception, a fertilized human egg is about the size of a pinhead, yet it contains information equivalent to about six billion chemical letters. This is enough information to fill 1,000 books, 500 pages thick with print so small you would need a microscope to read it! If all the chemical letters in the human body were printed in books, it is estimated they would fill the Grand Canyon fifty times!"[26]

The complexity of life points to the unavoidable conclusion that we are not the product of chance. We are the result of some force, power or being that is the ultimate cause for everything that exists, or at the very least guides the process.

---

24 www.khouse.org/enews_article/2006/1082/accessed January 18, 2008
25 Dawkins, Richard. The Blind Watchmaker WW Norton & Company, New York, London, 1987, 6
26 www.khouse.org/enews_article/2006/1082, accessed January 18, 2008 Paley, William, D.D. Public Domain 10802

Natural Selection: The Cause for All Things?

The theory of natural selection states that over long periods of time life evolved from a single cell into all kinds of life we see today. Is natural selection the cause for all living things? Dawkins believes it is and has assured us that natural selection is blind and does not make plans. So how are objects able to adapt?

> *"Natural selection, the blind, unconscious, automatic process which Darwin discovered, and which we now know is the explanation for the existence and apparently purposeful form of all life, has no purpose in mind. It has no mind and no mind's eye. It does not plan for the future. It has no vision, no foresight, and no sight at all."*[27]

According to Dawkins, natural selection occurs because of its need to survive. *"The cumulative process is directed by non-random survival."*[28] So this cumulative process is not random but a series of "right" choices.

What explanation can there be for natural selection or matter creating the environment needed for our survival? How or why would inanimate objects place themselves in just the right locations to support living things? Why does matter itself want to survive? If natural selection is blind and unplanned, how does it get anywhere? If it is not random, then it is directed.

In 1859, Charles Darwin wrote *The Origin of the Species.* For many scientists, natural selection (Darwin's theory of evolution) is the answer to the creationist philosophy of intelligent design. To understand fully his position on natural selection,

---

27 Dawkins, Richard. The Blind Watchmaker WW Norton & Company, New York, London, 1987, 5
28 IBID, pg. 43

it is best to see it in contrast with the philosophy of intelligent design.

Intelligent design is not really a new theory but an updated version of the argument from design held by many theists in history. William Paley's dissertation, "Natural Theology," is the classic treatise on intelligent design. Dawkins presents his philosophy of natural selection by contrasting it to Paley's intelligent design.

Paley then compares nature to the watch. His basic argument is that if you find a stone on the ground you would not question it being there. However, if you found a watch on the ground you would rightly assume it had a creator that caused it to be.[29]

Paley's basic argument is that is impossible to believe that life with its complexity could exist without the presence of a designer or watchmaker, an intelligent agent or cause for the universe.

In *The Blind Watchmaker*, Dawkins answers Paley's arguments. He believes natural selection is how the universe developed. He says,

Dawkin's response is that Paley is wrong: All appearances to the contrary, the only watchmaker in nature are the blind forces of physics, albeit deployed in a very special way. "Natural selection, the blind, unconscious, automatic process which Darwin discovered, and which we now know is the explanation for the existence and apparently purposeful form of all life has no purpose in mind. It has no mind and no mind's eye. It does not plan. It has no vision, no foresight, and no sight at all. If it can be said

---

29 en.wikipedia.org/wiki/Watchmaker_analogy

to play the role of watchmaker in nature, it is the blind watchmaker.

"We have seen that living things are too improbable and too beautifully designed to come into existence by chance. How, then, did they come into existence? Darwin's answer is, a gradual, step-by-step transformations from simple beginnings, from primordial entities sufficiently simple to have come into existence by chance.[30]

Dawkins claims to know the explanation. He claims to know this not because of the facts but because he has ruled out any other possibility. He utterly rejects a creator or any intelligent being as a cause.

Dawkins's prejudice and bias against the supernatural has blinded him to any objective truth on this topic. He is saying that natural selection is not only the cause for the purposefulness (complexity) of life but is somehow also responsible for the existence of life. He concedes that natural selection is a blind, mindless, purposeless and automatic process without foresight. He believes it cannot see or even consider what might happen in the future, yet somehow it is the cause for all life and complex life forms.

How does this blind, mindless, purposeless, automatic process work? By taking an unguided, unplanned and innumerable number of tiny steps over millions and millions of years for unknown reasons.

To suggest that an unknown, unseen and unplanned series of simple cumulative steps leads to a complex end is not an argument for random chance. Is it more difficult to take several

---

30 Dawkins, Richard. The Blind Watchmaker WW Norton & Company, New York, London, 1987, 5

Bridging the Origins Divide

large steps in the darkness than many small ones? You may miss a hole with a large step or fall into one with a small step.

If you find yourself in a pitch-black cave without a reference point, it makes no difference if you take thousands of tiny steps instead of hundreds of large steps. It makes no difference if you turn right instead of left or go up instead of down. In fact, it makes no difference what you do, since there is no plan in the first place. Is your purpose to get out of the cave or to stay inside? Without a plan or purpose, it does not matter if you get out or stay in. If you by chance came upon something interesting while inside, it would be meaningless because there was no forethought or purpose.

Without a design or purpose, natural selection is still a random process, regardless of any statements to the contrary. It can only be considered an incredible stroke of luck for evolution to reach any destination, especially one as lofty as the human being.

Natural Selection: A Process, Not a Cause

Natural selection is a theoretical process which deals primarily with the evolution of living matter. It is a theory that attempts to explain how living things move from simple to complex life forms.

As a scientific theory, it leaves many ideas unexplained such as the origin of the universe or living things. It cannot explain how the spark of life happened and how it survived in an extremely precarious environment. Natural selection cannot explain why there are so many different, fully developed, functioning species.

Micro vs. Macro Evolution

Natural selection is based primarily on the theory that microevolution (small changes within a given species) proves macroevolution (cross species mutation). Microevolution is nothing more than adaptation. Adaptation is the ability of a living thing to change as its environment changes. An animal's fur will change color in different environments. In the arctic, a fox is white; in the desert it is brown. This is quite different from a pig becoming a giraffe or a chimpanzee becoming a human being.

Cross species mutation is in direct conflict with the biblical record of creation. Genesis 1:11 and 1:21 reveal that "everything reproduces after its own kind." A biblical kind or species is defined as any being that can successfully produce offspring through mating.

There is no evidence that a species has ever transitioned to a new and different kind. Evolution's speculation of massive cross-species mutation is unproven and without evidence. Science believes it happens because it fits naturalistic assumptions concerning creation. Additionally, cross-species mutation fits their belief that similarity of design demonstrates macroevolution. However, it is more likely that design similarities speak of a single highly intelligent being who not only designed all living things but also provided them with the capacity to adapt to changing environments over long periods of time.

The process of adaptation within a specific species is logical. Environmental changes demand adaptation to survive. However, there is no reason for cross-species mutation; the elephant is quite capable of survival as an elephant. An elephant that evolves into a new species is not likely to survive in the new form as it was in the old. It would certainly be difficult to survive in a transitional form, so most likely it would not. In the case of bacteria. For example, adapting to antibiotics would not be evidence of a cross-species mutation.

It is the same with all species. There is no indication that any life form *must* change its basic form. Other than the need to explain complexity without a creator, there is no need for cross-species mutation. Does the chimpanzee desire to be human? Humans are more intelligent than chimpanzees, yet chimpanzees seem quite content in their own world. There are things they can do that we cannot; and in some situations, they might have a greater chance of survival than humans. The chimpanzees' feet are built for climbing trees much more easily than humans. Their long hair keeps them protected from the elements better than us.

Argument Five: Morality

Does absolute right and wrong exist? Are there absolute moral standards? Will human behavior be judged? Does our behavior have consequences? If so, how do we determine what is right and wrong? By whose standard do we mete out justice and judgment?

At the time of this writing, the world is engaged in a moral argument. Some support Hamas as freedom fighters combating the tyranny of Jewish occupation. They justify their actions—targeting civilians and beheading babies of Jewish descent—based on their moral standards. Others are outraged at the atrocities and demand the eradication of Hamas members and all terrorist groups. Who has the right to pass judgment on human actions? To be sure, what Hamas did was unconscionable and pure evil, but without the benefit of an eternal and just creator, it is only my opinion.

For example, one father may love and provide for his family while another abuses and neglects his family. Who is to say which father has the "right" values? While almost everyone would support the first father, it is just a matter of opinion without an objective source. Relativism says there is no absolute truth. Agnostic philosopher of science Michael Ruse said,

> *"The position of the modern evolutionist is that ... morality is a biological adaptation no less than hands and feet and teeth and ethics is illusory. I appreciate that when somebody says, 'Love thy neighbor as thyself,' they think they are referring above and beyond themselves. Nevertheless, such reference is truly without foundation. Morality is just an aid to survival and reproduction ... and any deeper meaning is illusory."*[31]

The only objective basis for morality must come from the one who made the laws of nature and of human interaction in which the universe operates. Not just the laws of nature, but the laws of human relationships.

On one hand, if all actions are equal and merit the same reward, and if our actions have no consequences, then life is without meaning. On the other hand, someone must determine the laws and constructs that protect us against murder, theft, adultery, pedophilia, assault, etc.

Apart from a creator there can be no objective morality. An atheist can live a relatively moral life, but there would not be an objective reason on which to base his beliefs. Only the one responsible for the world and humanity has the moral right to

---

31 Michael Ruse, "Evolutionary Theory and Christian Ethics," in the Darwinian Paradigm (London: Routledge, 1989), pp. 262-269)

Bridging the Origins Divide

set human standards and judge human actions. He is both the lawgiver and the judge.

Education and Science

If atheistic evolution is true, the beliefs about science and religion would be rendered completely irrelevant. It would not matter what a scientist says about the origin of life or what a church believes about a creator. Life would be nothing more than animated dust. *"All we are is dust in the wind."*[32]

Lawlessness and Anarchy Reign

The logical conclusion of atheistic evolution puts mankind on the brink of anarchy and chaos. If Stenger and others like him choose to believe life does not need meaning or purpose, that is their opinion. But is this a reasonable answer for the realities of human existence? People living in misery and poverty around the world would not appreciate being told their life has no meaning at all and that survival of the fittest is the only rule of the universe.

If survival of the fittest is an acceptable rule of life, get strong and just take what you want. Be nice to people only if it benefits you. Do whatever makes you happy. Eat, drink and be merry, for tomorrow we die. Having come from nothing, we will return to nothing.

Our One Hope

Humanity's one hope is that there is a creator and that he is good. We must have faith that someday the suffering and pain of life will make sense. To believe otherwise is to give into nihilism and a profound hopelessness for the future of mankind.

---

32   Dust in the Wind" written by Kerry Livgren,

We want to believe there is a creator who is greater and wiser than mankind and who will judge the actions of Earth's inhabitants. We need to know that those who murder, rape and steal will be punished. Those who claim not to care are not being honest with themselves. Perhaps they have given in to their own hopeless world view.

Chapter Three

Why It Matters

When I entered the dry sauna, a young man and a middle-aged woman were warming themselves. The woman's eyes were closed, and she was wearing earbuds. She may as well have had a sign on her forehead that read, "Please do not disturb." I decided to strike up a conversation with the young man. We spoke for about 15 minutes on the existence of God and other spiritual things. He believed in a creator and was very interested in the topic. When he was done, he stood up and left.

During this conversation, the woman never looked at me or gave any indication she was listening or interested in our topic. As soon as the young man left the room, I turned toward her and asked her what she thought about the conversation. To my surprise, she looked at me and said, "I do not believe in God."

We then began a dialogue on the merits of theism. About five minutes into our conversation, I changed my approach and asked her if anything had happened to her that may have influenced her non-belief in God. Her response floored me. She told me she was the only member of her family of eight who had survived a deadly car crash. Additionally, she had recently lost her 16-year-old son to cancer.

I was deeply moved by her story and found myself in the unusual position of having nothing to say. I prayed silently, asking the Lord for direction. In the end, I was led to tell her two things.

The first thing I said to her was that God did not cause the deaths of her family or son and that His plan was not for them to die that way. Secondly, I mentioned that God loved her very deeply, understood her pain and wanted to help her if she would let him. I then asked her if I could pray for her, and to my surprise she said yes. I prayed that God would heal her heart and that she would have a revelation of the love of Jesus in her life. She left, and I have not seen her since.

Doubt and non-belief can occur for different reasons. Non-belief may result from conflicts with science, a negative religious experience, deep pain and loss, or even from an influential teacher or mentor. Some may question why an all-powerful God allows evil in the world. Atheism is often a cover for a painful root cause which has affected a person's belief system.

Religious Indoctrination

One cannot separate atheism from religion; they are opposite sides of the same coin. Atheists almost always come from a religious background. In fact, atheism is often a reaction to overbearing or abusive religious institutions.

In his online article, *Religion's Real Child Abuse,* Richard Dawkins promotes the notion that the greatest abuse of children by the church is not rampant sexual abuse; rather it is the indoctrination of children into religious beliefs. The assumption by men like Dawkins is that belief in God is the result of religious brainwashing by "charismatic charlatans" found in religious institutions. We must not allow negative personal experiences to unduly influence the discussion about the existence of a creator.

Belief in a creator is based on observation and deduction, not on the behavior of religious leaders, the Bible, Quran or any other religious book. Religious books and institutions can play a role in this belief, but they are not foundational to it.

To answer a child's query about the universe with the words, *God made it,* is not religious indoctrination. It reflects the logical belief held by most of humanity concerning the existence of the universe and living things. Dawkins, Harris and other renowned atheists are attempting to indoctrinate children and anyone they can to their worldview. I affirm their right to do so; however, church leaders and philosophers have the same rights. It is not brainwashing to simply express one's beliefs.

Philip Pullman, author of *His Dark Materials,* is an atheist whose stated objective is to promote atheism and to "kill God in the minds of children."[33] He has stated that he despises C.S. Lewis and *The Chronicles of Narnia.* When pressed about his reasons for rejecting the existence of God, Pullman said,

> *"Well, all right, it comes from history. It comes from the record of the Inquisition, persecuting heretics and torturing Jews and all that sort of stuff; and it comes from the other side, too, from the Protestants burning the Catholics. It comes from the insensate pursuit of innocent and crazy old women, and from the Puritans in America burning and hanging the witches–and it comes not only from the Christian church but also from the Taliban."[34]*

---

33   goodreads.com/author/quotes3618.Philip_Pullman
34   IBID

His views reflect those of many atheists and agnostics. One has only to read *Letters from the Earth* by Mark Twain, *The God Delusion* by Richard Dawkins, or *Why I Am Not a Christian* by Bertrand Russell to see that a negative view of religion is shared by most atheists.

Admittedly, it would be almost impossible to tell the history of western civilization if we were to leave out references to religious wars, inquisitions, greed and corruption in the church. Sadly, many have forgotten the words of Jesus: "Love thy neighbor as thyself" and "Turn the other cheek." Instead of caring for the poor, some religious leaders have become wealthy at their expense.

There has been corruption within many religious organizations. The Catholic Inquisitions, contemporary Muslim Jihadists and overt racism within southern American churches have all made it difficult for some to believe in a good creator. Many professors at elite doctoral universities are hostile to religion, the Bible and the existence of a creator. The ease with which Christian Europe accepted Darwinism and schools of higher criticism are also evidence of a predominantly negative view of religion.

Individuals from every profession—actors, educators, governors and doctors to name a few—have betrayed the morality and values of their professions. They have abused and harmed the very people they were supposed to help. Scientists developed the drugs and chemical fertilizers that pollute the earth every day, not to mention creating almost every weapon known to mankind.

Nazi scientists performed experiments on human beings that no normal person would perform even on animals. Very few people have written books intended to undermine belief in science or its value to mankind.

It is especially grievous when religious people abuse others in His name. I recently spoke with two middle-aged men who had very negative histories with religious people. I could give them no satisfactory answer to placate their anger and disappointment. Their rejection of a creator was in part the direct observation of ungodly behavior by religious people. I was saddened for their sakes and embarrassed by their stories. However, we should remain objective and keep this in mind:

> *The existence or non-existence of a creator has nothing to do with the way religious people behave. The issue is not that religious people have failed to live up to the Creator's standards (which they certainly have). It is whether there is a creator who has standards to live up to.*

The Good of Religion

Though many religious leaders and their followers have been known to exhibit questionable behaviors, we should acknowledge the many good deeds that have been done in the name of religion. The existence of hospitals, universities and representative forms of government throughout history are great examples.

The same can be said for child literacy and education, a high regard for human life and for the existence of standards of justice. Civil rights and the eradication of slavery in America were driven by Christians and abolitionists preachers who held that all men were created equal in God's eyes.

In England, William Wilberforce fought for almost fifty years at great personal cost to see slavery outlawed and to avoid a civil war. Wilberforce based his defense on his Christian faith. Science was likely founded by believers who wanted to know the mind of the Creator.

Good and evil exist in every level of culture, profession and institution governed by human beings. Humans are the impetus for activity, and we have the potential for both good and evil. Belief in a creator is not an endorsement of religion or faith; it is simply a logical explanation for the existence of the universe.

Does it matter?

In the west, the long-term effects of atheism are often obscured by the prevalence of a biblical worldview engrained in most Western cultures. Unlike many other cultures, the West places a high value on altruism, human life, care for the poor, justice and freedom for all. An atheist in our society will practice these Christian values without hesitation or reflection as to their source. So… do good and evil exist, and are there eternal consequences for our actions?

How we answer these questions is critical. Some atheists are kind and live generally moral lives, but that does not negate the reality of the destructive nature of individuals who have no conscience or fear of judgment from an eternal creator.

The behavior of certain religious people throughout history pales in comparison to the morally reprehensible slaughter of human beings in the 20th century. The atheist Stalin murdered over 20 million of his own citizens without any consideration of the eventual judgment of a creator. Hitler murdered 6,000,000 Jews, and over 70 million people died in World War Two.

Hitler falsely claimed to be religious and a Christian, but like many manipulators he used God and religion as a tool. He was directly involved in the occult, which was the real power behind his behavior. He lived as an atheist and a man without a conscience, and he had no concern for a creator who would judge his actions.

What we believe about the existence and nature of a creator will have a profound impact on our life and the lives of those around us. If human beings are simply soulless entities—the random offspring of an unplanned, uncaused evolutionary process—then our actions do not really matter. When our bodies die and we cease to exist, and if there are no eternal consequences for our actions, then objective morality and meaning are simply constructions of mass guilt and manipulation by those in power.

If the creator is a disinterested entity or non-personal energy, then judgment of our actions is not relevant. However, if the creator is a personal being who cares about humanity and is intent on bringing justice to those who are mistreated and judgment to the guilty, it may curb the unbridled actions of evil individuals.

Chapter Four

Faith Versus Science

Is Faith Blind?

They say love is blind. For the scientific atheist, faith is blind. They consider that belief in God is based on blind faith separate from reason and scientific evidence. Science is rational. Belief in a creator is irrational and reserved for the weak-minded, emotional, easily duped and uneducated segment of society. The *Encarta World English Dictionary* defines faith as,

> *"Belief or trust; belief in, devotion to, or trust in somebody or something, especially without logical proof."*[35]

Friedrich Nietzsche said,

> *"Faith: not wanting to know what is true."*[36]

Richard Dawkins claimed,

> *Faith is the great cop-out, the great excuse to evade the*

---

35   The Encarta World English Dictionary, St. Martin's Press (August 1999
36   thinkexist.com/quotes/friedrich_nietzsche/

need to think and evaluate evidence. Faith is belief in spite of, even perhaps because of, the lack of evidence.[37]

Perhaps a better, less biased definition is *"complete trust or confidence in someone or something"* or *"a strongly held belief."* Without an investigation we cannot know why a person has faith or belief in something. We do not know what they are basing their faith on.

The Encarta dictionary definition is an incomplete definition of faith. Some individuals may believe in a creator without understanding the complexity of the arguments, but that does not mean they are wrong about a creator's existence.

The intent of all these definitions is to create an illusion of intellectualism for the atheist. They might say something like, "I have looked at the scientific evidence and there is no proof of a creator. You as the deceived believer are blindly following the irrational beliefs of religious charlatans." When spoken by professors in the classroom or other public forums, these definitions are used as a cudgel against those who believe in a creator. They are straw man arguments meant to paint theists as ignorant, non-thinking individuals.

The standard argument in its simplest form says everything has a cause, and the cause must be greater than its effect. This does not ignore the evidence but gives a rational explanation for the existence of a massive, complex universe filled with living things. However, faith is not blind, irrational or foolish. It is neither negative nor positive. It is merely an action or decision based on a belief. Your faith is only as good as the person or object you are placing it in.

---

37 www.goodreads.com/quotes/

Relativism

Agnostics offer another objection to the existence of a creator: no one really knows or can know for certain. While numerous variations on this theme abound, it comes down to the belief that there are no absolute truths. Friedrich Nietzsche, a highly influential German philosopher of the late 19th century and the father of relativism claimed that,

> *"God is dead,"[38] and "You have your way. I have my way. As for the right way, the correct way, and the only way, it does not exist."[39]*

Postmodernism and recent progressivism believe there is no absolute truth and that it is arrogant to claim one's beliefs are true. Philosophical and religious truths are cultural and a matter of opinion. In contemporary society, this has been fused with the belief that truth can be found only through the scientific method. The issue is further compounded by the current cultural demands of tolerance and globalism. Proponents claim all beliefs are equally worthy and that there is no absolute truth concerning religions, worldviews or even morality.

> *However, truth cannot be relative, subjective or a matter of opinion. Truth is absolute and is not affected by our personal feelings or beliefs. It is not a matter of what the majority thinks or believes, which political party is in power or who controls the airwaves. We may believe in something very sincerely, but it is only an opinion and not fact.*

A creator either does or does not exist; both things cannot be

---

38   The Gay Science (Die frohliche Wissenschaft, 1882) section 125)
39   www.goodreads.com/quotes

Bridging the Origins Divide

true. Absolute moral laws exist, or they do not. Furthermore, Nietzsche's statement, "*The right way, correct way or only way does not exist*," is an absolute statement and a contradiction. Logically, you cannot make an absolute statement about the non-existence of absolutes.

Every person and all societies have the freedom to believe whatever they want about morality, social taboos and religion. However, this does not mean everyone's beliefs are right. The idea of tolerance and respecting the beliefs of others is commendable; but this does not mean that there is no absolute truth, or that we should not discuss our differences.

Not every societal practice in every culture is good. From a moral perspective, some practices are relative, while others are absolute. Personal hairstyle and what you wear to the opera are relative choices; they are morally neutral. Someone may not like your hairstyle or what you wore to the opera, but it is clearly your choice and has no effect on significant issues. However, few would argue that the practice of blowing yourself up to kill your enemies should be accepted as an alternative lifestyle.

Scientific Atheism

The primary challenge to theism (belief in God) is scientific atheism (belief in no God). This belief has grown in recent years as militant scientific atheists grew bolder and more assertive in their claims concerning evolution. In the minds of many of these scientists, evolution (natural selection) is not a theory at all but an established fact.

They believe that the big bang and natural selection are sufficient explanations for the creation of the universe. They believe there is no need for a personal creator and that everything we see in the universe can be adequately explained by a natural process. Because these statements come from respected scientists, they carry a great deal of authority and have brought confusion and doubt to many. The absolute nature of their claims is based on the underlying belief in anti-supernaturalism. If the supernatural realm does not align with that belief, the creation of all things must be found in the natural world.

It is not surprising that some of these scientists have placed themselves in the role of "answer men" to all of society's questions. The line between science and philosophy was blurred. Scientists took inconclusive data and drew absolute conclusions from it. Richard Dawkins, author of *The Blind Watchmaker* and *The God Delusion*, said,

> *"An atheist before* Darwin's Origin of Species *was published could have said, following Hume: I have no explanation for complex biological design. All I know is that God isn't a good explanation, so we must wait and hope that somebody comes up with a better one."*[40]

As a result, Dawkins concluded that *"Darwin has made it possible to be an intellectually fulfilled atheist."*[41] He continues,

> *"You cannot be both sane and well educated and disbelieve in evolution. The evidence is so strong that any sane, educated person must believe in evolution. It is safe to say that, if you meet somebody who claims not to believe in evolution, that person is ignorant, stupid or insane."*[42]

The late Carl Sagan said,

> *"Since the birth of the universe could now be explained*

---

40   Dawkins, Richard. The Blind Watchmaker WW Norton & Company, New York, London, 1987, .6
41   IBID
42   IBID

by the laws of physics alone … he concluded there was
nothing for a creator to do, and every thinking person
was therefore forced to admit the absence of God."[43]

The good news is that this is slowly changing. Richard Dawkins, an avowed outspoken atheist, has raised eyebrows after describing himself as an agnostic and admitting he cannot disprove the existence of God.[44]

Making Contact

In 1985, a best-selling novel by Carl Sagan evolved into the movie *Contact*. Sagan often uses his books and videos to mock people who believe in a creator while simultaneously portraying scientists as misunderstood heroes and the lone seekers of truth.

Jodie Foster plays Ellie Arroway, a brilliant scientist who lost both parents in childhood. In Sunday school, she asked too many tough questions and was asked to leave. Consequently, she had no place for faith or religion. When pressed about her belief in God, she said,

"I am a scientist, and I need empirical evidence. I don't
have the luxury of faith; besides, there is no data support-
ing the existence of a Creator."[45]

Matthew McConaughey plays Palmer Joss, a religious scholar and top-level government advisor. He makes it clear that his faith is based on an experience that changed his life. While he considered himself reasonably intelligent, the experience was far beyond his capacity. Overall, Sagan's message regarding people of faith is that belief in a creator is an emotional belief without logic or reason.

---

43   Sagan, Carl. Contact, Warner Bros. studios, 1997
44   theweek.com/religion/religion/45552
45   Sagan, Carl. Contact, Warner Bros. studios, 1997

In the movie, McConaughey's character failed to realize the empirical evidence for creation is heaven, earth and its millions of living entities. Foster is confusing ancient Greek deities with an eternal and invisible creator who is no longer creating, having finished those activities long ago.

Scientific Intimidation

In conjunction with Dawkins' and Sagan's rhetoric about faith, scientists use these types of stereotypical portrayals to confuse many people. Even fellow scientists find themselves intimidated into going along with these so-called great thinkers. Scientist and life-long atheist Allan Sandage recently converted to theism and confessed,

> *"Today the scientific community scorns faith so much that there is a reluctance to reveal yourself as a believer, the opprobrium [contempt] is so severe."*[46]

If scientists such as Dr. Sandage are intimidated, is it understandable that many in society are as well. The use of technical jargon along with dogmatism often leaves a reader confused, feeling ignorant and afraid to even raise an objection.

Science is not the problem.

Religion is not anti-science, and neither is this book. Creationism and science are not incompatible. Scientists have discovered many wonderful things. The technological advances of the 20th and 21st centuries are remarkable. There is nothing wrong with the scientific method or the study of life and origins. However, scientists are limited in what they know and understand.

As Dr. Kaku has said, the scientific method cannot deter-

46　Begley, Sharon/ Westley, Marian. Newsweek, Volume 132, Issue 3 July 20, 1998. Science Finds God

mine the existence of a creator. It cannot tell us with certainty how the heavens and earth were created. Science is limited to examination of what *is,* not how it all came to be. Scientists can only speculate about origin and history. However, no experiments or tests can be performed on the original creation of the universe. All scientific theories concerning the origin of the universe are speculative and not factual.

Scientific research is limited to the natural world. A supernatural world is not subject to the natural world. Thus, any supernatural cause or intervention into the natural realm would skew any observed data. For instance, the apparent age of the universe could have a completely different foundation than what we have ever considered.

Is science objective?

Distrust of authority became an art form in the 1960s. Over the years, many leaders have been caught lying and stealing. They've been involved in sexual immorality and so much political corruption that it's easy to be jaded about their integrity.

However, when a scientist speaks, his views are generally accepted as absolute truth and rarely questioned or scrutinized. I am not accusing scientists of being dishonest, but we need to understand they operate on presuppositions that affect their objectivity. These presuppositions color their view of the given data and often hinder objective interpretation of their observations.

Beyond the conflict between creationism and evolution is a much broader problem. In the film, *Expelled,* Ben Stein interviewed numerous scientists who had lost their positions in the academic world because they had written about or brought up the topic of intelligent design.

The problem appears to be widespread in universities and

leading scientific institutions. The perpetrators of these metaphorical book burnings were adamant in their rejection and revulsion of any suggestion that there could be a supernatural cause for the universe. They were clearly biased and denigrated anyone who dared disagree with their views of evolution.

Ironically, theists and others who simply want to discuss their beliefs are deemed radical fundamentalists and placed in the same company as Islamic extremists. An even greater irony is that science owes its very existence to theists. It was Christian theists who believed a creator had made the universe in an orderly fashion to begin with.

"My astronomy research is merely thinking God's thoughts after Him."[47]

—Johann Kepler

"The more I study nature, the more I stand amazed at the work of the Creator."[48]

—Louis Pasteur

"Science without religion is lame; religion without science is blind."[49]

—Albert Einstein

"It is the perfection of God's works that they are all done with the greatest simplicity. He is the God of order and not of confusion."[50]

—Isaac Newton

---

47 Attributed to Johanna Kepler,
48 Stated in a speech near the end of his life. www.answersingenesis.org/contents/379/Louis-Pasteur.pdf
49 www.theguardian.com/science
50 Rules for methodizing the Apocalypse, Rule 9, from a manuscript published in The Religion of Isaac Newton (1974) by Frank E. Manuel, p. 120

          Bridging the Origins Divide

These men and many others like them believed in a creator. They approached their study from a different worldview than many of today's scientists.

Scientific Presuppositions

Everyone has presuppositions, These are underlying assumptions that affect how we view data. Scientists are no different, and they approach with bias the data surrounding our origins. The goal is to determine if these presuppositions are accurate.

The primary belief system of science is naturalism. This is the belief that everything can be understood through a natural process. The scientific method is based on natural laws and repeatable processes. However, when it comes to creation, scientific naturalism proposes creation without supernatural involvement. In other words, they begin with a bias that the origin of the universe and all living things must be explained by a natural process which cannot appeal to supernatural activity.

Naturalism has been the predominant belief system among scientists and philosophers for at least 150 years, and it has influenced many to forsake traditional religions. Regarding the origin of the earth, naturalism means creation without supernatural involvement. It claims the earth was formed by a natural process without miracles or supernatural activity.

"Naturalism is any of several philosophical stances ... descended from materialism and pragmatism ... Naturalism does not necessarily claim that phenomena or hypotheses commonly labeled as supernatural do not exist or are wrong but insists that all phenomena and hypotheses can be studied by the same methods and therefore anything considered supernatural is either non-

Thus, the supernatural may exist, but it can only be known by a natural process that can be tested empirically. However, any event that can be tested in the natural world is not supernatural. By this reckoning, naturalism is inherently anti-supernatural. Even to theistic scientists, naturalism would still be the lens through which they examine the universe. It is their primary philosophical basis for evolution.

Scientific commitment to naturalism and natural selection causes scientists to devote all or most of their time and energy to the defense of anti-supernatural assumptions. This creates a barrier between religion and science. For any scientist to acknowledge the existence of the supernatural is a career-ending proposition. Scientist Alan Sandage willed himself to accept God:

"It was my science that drove me to the conclusion that the world is much more complicated than can be explained by science. It is only through the supernatural that I can understand the mystery of existence."[52]

The commitment to naturalism is so strong in a scientific worldview that Dr. Sandage had to force himself to change his mind. Dawkins' adherence to naturalism has led him to define miracles in this way:

"Miracles are not supernatural but are part of a spectrum of more-or-less improbable natural events. A miracle, in

---

51 Wikipedia Online Dictionary en.wikipediaorg/wiki/Intelligent_design, accessed Feb.3, 2008

52 Begley, Sharon/ Westley, Marian. Newsweek, Volume 132, Issue 3 July 20, 1998. Science Finds God.

other words, if it occurs at all, is not really a miracle, but
a tremendous stroke of luck."[53]

His definition locks Dawkins in a philosophic closet from which he cannot clearly see reality. His commitment to naturalism only allows him to see the world as he believes it to be. Hence, according to his definition, there is no possibility of a supernatural explanation for the universe.

The contradictory beliefs concerning miracles are based on assumptions about the existence of a creator. A miracle is quite a simple thing for a being that created the entire universe from nothing. However, if you reject the possibility of a creator and hold only to anti-supernatural suppositions, you arrive at only a natural explanation.

Summary: We Know There Is a Creator

"Belief in a creator is a self-evident truth understood through reason. It is not blind faith or religious indoctrination."

Belief in a creator is a philosophical question for which science has no answer. Investigation into the existence of a creator must begin with an open mind and proper suppositions, not the bias of naturalism.

The state of nothingness cannot produce something; therefore, someone or something has always existed. Everything else must be causative. Given that structured matter and complex life forms exist, they must have been caused.

"The universe and life forms are far too complex to have been caused by random chance."

Natural selection and the big bang are processes, not causes. They could not create the universe or simple or complex life

---

53 Dawkins, Richard. The Blind Watchmaker WW Norton & Company, New York, London, 1987, 139

forms. They, too, would be dependent on an eternal power as their source.

Human beings are of infinite value. If matter or natural selection were the creator, then nothing would matter at all. Human beings and all life forms would be animated dust without purpose.

Human decisions have eternal consequences. If matter or natural selection were the Creator, then there is no basis for morality, and therefore every action is equally valid. Murder and rape would be as valuable as love and protection. What we do would be utterly insignificant and without meaning.

The following story serves as an illustration of our belief in a Creator. While I am not a Trekkie, I watched many episodes of *Star Trek*. In one episode, *Spectre of the Gun,* several crew members were transported to a planet against their will by a race called the Melkotians. To us, the crew looked normal, but in the Tombstone, Arizona locale, the people saw Ike Clanton, Tom McCloury, Billy Clanton and Frank McClary.

They were forced to participate in the infamous gunfight at the OK Corral. The men desperately sought ways to avoid the battle. If the historic parallel was to be fulfilled, most of them would die. Dr. McCoy concocted a knockout gas using a chemical formula which Spock tested on himself. When they saw it had no effect, the crew realized everything they were experiencing was an illusion. Nothing could harm them if they *believed* that. Spock stated with certainty,

> *"Physical reality is consistent with universal laws. Where the laws do not operate, there is no reality—we judge reality by the responses of our senses. Once we are convinced of the reality of a given situation, we abide by its rules ...*

Physical laws simply cannot be ignored. Existence cannot be without them."

Using a mind meld, Spock convinced everyone that nothing around them was real, especially the bullets. They were all spared and eventually released from their captors.

That television episode serves as an appropriate analogy. When all possible conclusions are exhausted, the only option that remains for the creation of heaven, earth, simple and complex life forms is a creator. All created things are dependent on an eternal someone or power as their source. The creator is infinite and was never created. It is the only possible solution to our existence.

To deny the existence of a creator is like saying Mount Rushmore sculptor Gutzon Borglum came into existence on his own out of nothing. Carving this incredible monument took foresight, planning, organization, great intelligence and skill. It does not make sense to say that the universe and life are less complex than the carving of this monument.

Chapter Five

The Nature of the Creator

What is the creator like?

Every argument that has been made against the creator and subsequent basis for morality is a positive argument concerning the nature of a creator. Given that something always existed and that matter was at least shaped by a creator, it would also be true that the creator is eternal and has always existed.

The Creator As an Eternal Being

Having demonstrated that the existence of a creator is the only rational explanation for the universe, we can examine what we perceive or know about this creator. The nature of the universe implies various aspects of the capabilities, personality and character.

Whenever an argument for the existence of God is made, it is often challenged with *Where did God come from?* Let me remind you what Victor Stenger said:

"God is a different 'logical type' than the universe— a

type that does not require creation. Theologians do not make clear why the universe itself cannot be of this logical type."[54]

Dawkins considers belief in a creator a lazy explanation:

"Any God capable of intelligently designing something as complex as the DNA/protein replicating machine must have been at least as complex and organized as that machine itself. Far more so, if we suppose him additionally capable of such advanced functions as listening to prayer and forgiving sins.

"To explain the origin of the DNA/Protein machine by invoking a supernatural Designer is to explain precisely nothing, for it leaves unexplained the origin of the Designer. You have to say something like 'God was always there' and if you allow yourself that kind of lazy way out, you might as well just say DNA was always there, or Life was always there, and be done with it".[55]

Dawkins, like Stenger, implies there is no answer to God's origin; therefore, their postulations are as valid as others. However, the existence of an eternal and all-powerful creator remains the only logical explanation for the existence of the universe and complex life forms.

The creator is powerful and intelligent.

The heavens are immense. There are incredible amounts of energy beyond our capacity to comprehend. Our sun is 93 million miles away from us. It would take seven months to travel

---

54 Stenger,Victor. www.secularhumanism.org/library/fi
55 Dawkins, Richard. The Blind Watchmaker WW Norton & Company, New York, London, 1987, 141

there in today's space shuttle. The Pleiades star cluster is 400 light years away. It would take 70,000 years to reach that system. The Milky Way is so large that it would take 100,000 years to cross at the speed of light. To reach further galaxies would take millions of years.[56]

A star is a massive gaseous body. It generates energy through nuclear fusion and emits light. Our sun is also a star, but it is close enough to Earth to appear as a disk which provides us daylight.

Stars range in size from that of a city to 1,000 times larger than our sun. At one time, astronomers estimated there were at least 70 sextillion stars in the known universe. That is 230 billion times as many as the 300 billion in our own Milky Way. Following the discoveries of the Webb telescope, that number is now in septillions.[57]

The tremendous force required to move stars and planets into outer space is a clear demonstration of the Creator's power. When contrasted with human capacity, His power is magnified exponentially.

Smart Seeds

Can you make a tree? We can certainly create the shape of a tree using concrete, rubber or plastic, but it cannot grow or reproduce. If any part of this fake tree falls to the ground, it will not grow into another tree.

We can shape seeds that appear to be from an apple tree; but if planted in the ground, they will not produce an apple tree. The Creator made a smart tree and smart seed that contains all the necessary elements and capabilities of reproduction. One seed can produce innumerable trees.

---

56   www.harvard.edu/seuforum/howfar/sun
57   www.google.com/search?q=how+many+stars+are+in+the+universe

                                              Bridging the Origins Divide

The Creator is a person.

Humans and animals have their own unique bodies. When we describe the Creator as a person, we are describing a being who does not have a physical form. God is a spirit, a non-corporeal being. This is significant because all living things are composed of matter. If the Creator was a person with a human body, then that Creator would have had to be created.[58]

A human is rational, moral and self-aware. We possess the ability to relate meaningfully with other similar beings. Intelligence, morality and will are primary traits of human beings.

These inherent abilities separate humanity from the animal kingdom. It follows that the Creator must be equal to or greater than his creations, so these qualities must also exist in Him. There is correlation between justice, value and personality. We are aware of these traits, and they have meaning to us.

All living things have basic needs required for survival. A plant needs sunlight and water, but it is not offended if it does not receive what it needs; it just dies. A rock cannot appreciate the beauty of a sunrise or sunset, and it cannot tell the difference between summer and winter, kindness or cruelty, love or hate.

Animals can relate to humans on various levels. They can be trained to do various tasks, and they generally respond well to positive treatment from their owners, but they are clearly different from humans. They have no ability for abstract thoughts such as *Why do I exist?* or *What is the purpose of my life?* It is highly unlikely that a dog or a dolphin can appreciate the beauty of a sunset or a flower garden.

---

58 To clarify who Jesus is, he is the Creator, he is the God/Man, meaning that He is both deity and an eternal spirit, joined to a human body. So, in one sense God has a body, only because He created a human body to host His spirit.

Millions of people visit Sea World and are amazed at the sight of Shamu the whale when he carries a trainer on his back. They are enthralled with his power and speed as he races around the pool and splashes the audience. Few things compare to the thrill of seeing a pod of dolphins speed past us on the open sea. We have the capacity to enjoy and interact with created things because we are human.

It is reasonable to believe that the designer of the universe also cares about his creations. He must certainly be pleased and proud of what he has made. Conversely, it would be logical to assume he would be unhappy when his creations are abused or destroyed.

The Creator is just.

Justice and judgment are extremely uncomfortable concepts, especially in the realm of religion or philosophy. They carry negative and harsh connotations for most people. Most have experienced the need for justice at some point in their lives, and we have all made judgments. We judge the service and food quality at our favorite restaurant. We judge those who lead us, instruct our children, cut our hair and fix our cars. If we are not treated properly, we immediately cry foul and ask for justice.

We are also judged by the quality of our work, how we dress, how we relate with co-workers, how much money we make and where we live. When we make a judgment, it feels equitable and necessary. However, no one likes to *be* judged, especially in a negative manner.

The Need for Justice

Imagine what it would be like if you were never judged and never received any acknowledgment for your hard work and sacrifice or for the good things you do for others. Judgment is the only way we can be affirmed and thanked for our accomplishments. It is the only way to make improvements along the way.

Socialism and communism inherently fail because they are predicated on everyone receiving benefits regardless of individual contribution. Equal reward for inequality of work is unfair and self-defeating. Likewise, if the Creator never judged us for our actions, they would be meaningless and irrelevant, even for those we considered favorable.

Choices and consequences give our lives meaning and purpose. We all want to be successful and loved. Ultimately, judgment is a statement about the choices we have made and how they turned out.

If a thief steals garbage we have thrown out, we will not demand justice for what he took. We may be concerned he is around our house or that he may make a mess; but since we no longer value what we threw away, we would let it go. However, if he enters our house and steals our prized possessions or harms our children or spouse, we will demand he be arrested and that we receive justice.

Humans have the capacity to care about the world we live in. While most of us have no personal stake in buffaloes or whales, it grieves us to see them senselessly slaughtered. Most parents love and care for their children and would grieve any loss to the end of their days. Similarly, an artist treasures his masterpiece and would be deeply saddened if it were stolen or destroyed.

Imagine you are a husband and father of three children. One day you meet a homeless man who also is a father and husband. Out of the kindness of your heart, you take his family home to live with you. You set up house rules and explain them to both families.

Everyone cleans up after themselves and helps with designated chores. Any money the new family receives goes toward mutual expenses or is saved for a deposit for their own place. There will be no smoking, drugs or alcohol, and the adults must actively look for work.

After a short while, the visiting family decides to ignore the rules. They never clean up after themselves, they put holes in walls and stain the carpet. They keep everyone up at night and use their money to buy video games and alcohol. They also mistreat your own family.

One day, you find them next door with your alcoholic and irresponsible neighbor who always talks negatively about you and your family. Your house guest sings praises about your deadbeat neighbor but has never bothered to thank you for your hospitality. He simply expects you to continue to provide shelter for him and his family.

How would you respond to this situation? Would you continue to allow them to behave this way, or would you reiterate the boundaries and hope they follow them this time? Ultimately, you must judge them and tell them to leave if they refuse. You would do this for the sake of your family and your integrity.

The obvious analogy is that the Creator, who owns everything and gives us life and good things, also has the right to judge. Certainly, He has been very patient with humanity. When we murder and rape one another, He continues to feed and clothe us. He has not destroyed us, even though we are ungrateful for His provision and worship others instead of Him.

Bridging the Origins Divide

Is the Creator evil?

To believe the world is inherently evil is to believe its source is also evil and that the Creator's intention is for humanity to suffer. The idea that the universe could be run by an all-powerful, all-knowing, schizophrenic evil being is terrifying and makes no sense at all.

Not only would there be no hope and no reason to live, you might also hope there is no afterlife with such a being. It would be as if we lived in a never-ending horror movie.

Furthermore, why would an evil being create beautiful things? Evil is the distortion of something good or the misuse of an object or living thing. Evil is a resultant action caused by people's attitudes or beliefs. Evil does not create anything; it only causes chaos and destruction. Sadness and misery are its constant companions.

The Creator is good.

Is the Creator good or evil? If He is good, then what is the source of evil? If He is good and all-powerful, then why does He allow evil in the world? The philosopher Epicurus said it well:

"Either God wants to abolish evil, and cannot; or he can, but does not want to; or he cannot and does not want to. If he wants to, but cannot, he is impotent. If he can, and does not want to, he is wicked. But, if God both can and wants to abolish evil, then how comes evil in the world?"[59]

There are four possibilities to this aspect of the Creator's nature. He is either good, evil, has a split personality, or there are multiple creators.

Is the universe a bad place where good things happen occa-

---

59 Epicurus (341–270 B.C.), 2000 Years of Disbelief

sionally, or is it a good place where terrible things happen occasionally? From a strictly subjective point of view, our present daily experiences may influence our answer. If it is a good day, we think all is right with the world; on a dreadful day, we may think the opposite. However, if we view life optimistically, then the universe is a good place where terrible things happen occasionally.

Are there two Creators?

One possible explanation for the existence of evil and an all-powerful creator could be two gods. The ancient Greeks, Romans and other civilizations believed in many gods who were constantly at war with each other. It appeared there was a constant battle between equally powerful deities (good and evil). Humanity seemed to be at the mercy of their "mood swings."

The idea of two equal creators, one evil and one good, leads us to the same hopelessness and paranoia as an evil creator and should be rejected. Evil is the antithesis of good; it is the perversion of good. An evil creator is a paradox; its evil nature would preclude it from the creation of anything that could be considered good.

The evidence from the natural world shows there is one creator, not many. DNA in all living things is an indication of a single creator. Science believes the presence of DNA in all living things is indicative of evolution, but it can just as easily point to the existence of a single creator. This is clearly demonstrated in a *TIME* magazine article from October 8, 2006. On the cover is a chimpanzee and a human baby along with the title, "How We Became Human." It reveals that chimps and humans share almost 99% of their DNA.

According to the article, an artist had rendered a half-man,

Bridging the Origins Divide

half-monkey face. The point of the article was clear: the writer believes that human beings are directly descended from chimpanzees. He said that modern humans, like the great apes, are primates and part of an extended family tree that includes more than 275 living species.

The writer states this chimpanzee-human connection as fact. However, it is a conclusion based solely on the theory of evolution and naturalism. Humanity may share DNA with chimpanzees, but that does not mean we evolved from them.

It is more likely that DNA is how all life was created. It would then be a signature or trademark of a creator, which is a strong indication that one being designed and created all living things.

An art expert can determine whether a painting is a copy or an original. He can even discern the painter by the techniques used. The same is true of creation. Similarity of design does not demonstrate evolution, but it does indicate a single creator.

Free Will

If God wanted to be known and loved by His creations—especially humanity—he had to enable us to obey or disobey without coercion. The choices we make must be ours, even if our decisions cause us or others harm.

In the movie, *Bruce Almighty,* the following exchange takes place between Bruce (Jim Carrey) and God (Morgan Freeman): Bruce asks, "How do you make people love you without affecting free will?" God replies, "Welcome to my world, son. If you come up with an answer to that one, let me know."[60]

From a human perspective, this appears to create a dilemma: how does God allow freedom of choice and still accomplish

---

60   Bruce Almighty; Universal Pictures

what is best for humanity? He must allow us to choose whether to love or reject Him without coercion. If He gives us everything we want without consequences, we will gladly trust Him. However, this would not mean the relationship is trustworthy.

Most people would like to be friends with a rich person. Assume for a moment you are one of the richest and most powerful people on the planet. How do you choose your spouse and friends? How do you know they love you for more than just your money? How do you trust anyone to be your friend for who you are and not for what they can get from you?

You might wish to create a situation in which your full identity is hidden from a prospective suitor. You might conceal your identity so you could get to know someone without the pressure or influence of your fame and fortune. This is not unlike the challenge a creator would face.

Theologians and philosophers have debated the issue of free will for thousands of years. The viewpoints and complexities are many and too broad to be discussed here. Nevertheless, free will is an integral part of our relationship with each other and the Creator.

Many philosophers are determinists; that is, they believe an outside force is responsible for everything we do. This force entails a series of automatic responses—physical, psychological, biological and theological. Humanity is merely a product of his environment.

There are also other factors which influence our decisions. However, without the ability to choose one's own actions, there can be no true relationship with one another or with the Creator.

To say we are strictly the product of our environment

means that we are not responsible for our actions. Any judgment brought against us would in essence be unfair. If the Creator determines how we will behave, then we have no say in the matter and should not be held accountable. If He then judges us for actions He predetermined, then the Creator is not good but evil. All roads lead us back to free will. We are free moral agents and responsible for the choices we make.

Shared Accountability

The flipside of personal responsibility is shared accountability. We all play a role in the actions of those we have influenced. Your choices are affected by my actions and vice versa, thus we have a shared responsibility for the condition of the world.

An abused child is a victim of a failed parent/child relationship. If they grow up and abuse others, they must be held accountable for the decisions they make. We *understand* they were directly influenced by what was done to them, but it does not *excuse* their actions.

Most of us underestimate the impact of free will. We find it hard to imagine how our decisions or actions can make a difference. We find it difficult to believe the Creator cares about us or desires to have any relationship with us.

Our need for meaning and purpose implies that the Creator not only desires to have a relationship with us but also reveals that our actions and decisions are important. We can deduce that life without choice has no purpose, choices without consequences are meaningless, and life without judgment is worthless.

We are the problem.

Wars, murder, rape and racism are the result of human choices.

It is unreasonable to blame the Creator for the decisions people make. If a bullet is deliberately fired at someone, it is not done with unseen hands. A real person discharged the gun through free will.

Even accidents are the result of seemingly unrelated chains of events. Human error in a thousand diverse ways can lead to untold amounts of human suffering. We want the world to be perfect and for God to automatically protect everyone, but that would remove human choice.

If you want goodness, you must plan for evil. Both good and evil flow from the same source—the human soul.

> *"Where there are no oxen, the manger is empty [clean], but from the strength of an ox comes an abundant harvest."*
>
> —Proverbs 14:4.

The Value of Suffering

We grow stronger and become more humble and useful human beings when we experience difficulties. Imagine the problems humanity would face if we all had everything we wanted at any time.

In *Bruce Almighty,* the title character was temporarily given God's powers. He was quickly overwhelmed by the number of prayers and took the easy way out by saying yes to everyone. The result was chaos and pandemonium. In one example, his future sister-in-law won the lottery, but so did many others, and she only received about $17.

We are not smart enough to understand all the factors that influence the course of a person's life. We do not know what each person must experience in life to be who they are meant to be.

All suffering is not evil. Anyone who has ever accomplished a great task in the face of insurmountable odds knows the incredible joy of crossing the finish line. Suffering makes us strong. Soldiers are placed in stressful situations during training to prepare them for the realities they will face in warfare.

The same is true for all of us. Free will can lead to bad choices, which inevitably will produce suffering for humanity, but suffering can prepare us for life.

Suffering can bring us together.

There is value for individuals who are suffering. It can have a positive impact on those who observe and care for them. Depending upon the degree, it can be gratifying to care for those with physical or mental handicaps. Caregivers often realize they receive as much as they give. It can help us appreciate what we have when we give of our own selves.

If there is no creator to eventually make things right, then suffering is no different than not suffering. Jesus said:

"But many who are first will be last; and last, first." —Mathew *20:16.*

Things are likely to appear quite different in the future. Only an eternal creator can solve the issues which are beyond our capacity. What we can know for sure is that the Creator is good and not a source of evil.

The Creator is a communicator.

When people decide to have children, they inherently obligate themselves to take care of and provide for them. They are responsible for preparing them to get along in the world. In this way, the Creator is also obligated to his creations. Anything less would imply the Creator is evil.

A teacher would not be respectable if she gave a test on material the class was never taught or told to prepare for. People in authority obligate themselves to treat everyone fairly and honestly. We would consider any other behavior dishonest and wrong.

We need to know why we are here and what is expected of us. Since life matters, our actions are critically important. Our decisions affect our lives and the lives of those around us. We need to know what is right and wrong and what is harmful and safe.

The universe and human interaction are governed by rules put in place by the Creator. He knows how things work, and we need Him to tell us how things are. This would imply that somewhere on earth and within our reach is a book, religion or philosophy of life which instructs us in proper behavior. It would have the answers to our primary questions concerning the meaning and purpose of life.

Chapter Six

Who is the Creator?

During a conversation about the existence of God, a man once remarked, "You may be able to prove there is some sort of creator, but that does not mean it is the God of the Bible." This is true.

We have a working definition of God as an eternal, powerful and highly intelligent creator who has communicated to humanity. However, we have not identified who the creator is or how he has communicated with us. This serves as a point of reference. There is no question that the God of the Bible fits this description. However, the description is also found in several major religions.

It is not necessary to perform an exhaustive investigation into every religion on earth. Let's begin with the five major world religions: Buddhism, Christianity, Hinduism, Islam and Judaism. The following chart can be used as a comparison to each. It can also be used to compare other religions with respect to these characteristics.

God's Nature	Buddhism No God	Christianity	Hinduism	Islam	Judaism
Creator		•	•	•	•
Oneness		•	?	•	•
Eternal		•	•	•	•
Powerful		•	•	•	•
Intelligent		•	•	•	•
Good		•	?	?	•
Just		•	?	?	•
Person		•	?	?	•
Communicator		•	•	•	•

The *Pali Tripitaka* (Three Baskets) forms the foundation of Theravada Buddhism. The *Tripitakan* texts (scriptures) consist of the *Vinaya, Sutta* and *Abhidhamma*. For the most part, they apply to rules of conduct which govern daily affairs and to the nature of mind and matter. Buddhists do not believe in God. Presently, they accept the teaching of evolution to explain the existence of the universe. However, the four other religions above share our working definition of God.

This working explanation for a creator did not come from any religious source but from reason. However, it remains quite congruent with three of the other four religions. They share the same foundational source from which their understanding of God derives.

Judaism and Christianity have their roots in the Bible. The basic difference between Judaism and Christianity is the belief in Jesus as the Jewish Messiah. Christianity believes He was, while Judaism does not.

The primary teachings of Islam are based on the *Quran*. Muslims believe the Bible contains the words of God but that parts of it were corrupted by Mohammed's time around 600 AD. It is not surprising that they share a similar view of God as the creator.

   Bridging the Origins Divide

Hinduism is based primarily on the teachings of the *Bhaga-vad-Gita*. Without the influence of the Bible, it is interesting that the Hindus have come to a similar definition of the ultimate creator. Hindus are polytheistic, believing in many gods; however, they also believe in a supreme being—one God above all other gods.

The above religions also share in other areas of agreement such as the Ten Commandments. There are small differences in the way the commandments are communicated, but they are essentially the same. For example, they form the basis for civil laws in almost all societies and are practically universal in their acceptance among religions.

Why the Bible?

There are significant areas of disagreement that cannot be disregarded by simply claiming all religions are the same. Each has a different understanding of what it means to know, obey or please the creator.

Belief in a creator does not change a person's life or make them religious. Being religious does not mean you are following the precepts and meeting his expectations.

However, without a compelling reason to embrace one religion over another, the differences between them are simply matters of opinion. If one of these books is the Creator's message to humanity, it should be accepted by all people regardless of their religion, culture or personal belief.

Prophecy and the Bible

The most compelling argument for the Bible being God's word is the prophetic nature of the Bible. The ability to speak accurately and clearly concerning future events requires a supernatural source. It must be an eternal source that exists beyond the confines of time and human limitations.

The only source that can operate at this level is the eternal Creator, a being who knows all things, past, present and future and can see from the beginning to the end. From the ground, we cannot see a small town's boundaries from our point of view. However, if we observe above from a helicopter, it becomes very apparent. Similarly, the Creator exists beyond our observation and knows the beginning and end of all things.

The writers of the Bible claim the Creator spoke to them the words they wrote. Most of the forty-plus authors who wrote sections of the Bible claimed a supernatural encounter with God. The accurate fulfillment of prophecies supports their claim. We will briefly examine a few.

There are many reasons to believe the Bible is the Creator's message to mankind. Six are listed below. Since it is not the primary focus of this book, at this point we will only briefly discuss two.

- the uniqueness of the Bible
- the historical accuracy of the Bible
- the message of the Bible
- fulfilled prophecies about historical events
- fulfilled prophecies about the life of Jesus
- the resurrection of Jesus from the dead

Prophecies About Jesus

There are over 300 prophecies about Jesus. Of 61 major prophecies, 29 were fulfilled in a single day. They spoke of who His parents and great-grandparent would be, where He would be born and the way He would die. Many were prophecies that would have been impossible for Jesus to manipulate throughout His life. The chart below lists some of the prophecies found in the Bible about Jesus.

Born of a Woman	He would teach in Parables
Born of a Virgin	Sold for 30 Pieces of Silver
Son of Abraham	Accused by False Witnesses
Son of Isaac	Was silent in His defense
Son of Jacob	He would be beaten and spit on
Of the Tribe of Judah	He would be crucified
The Family Line of Jesse	His side would be pierced
The House of David	They would gamble for his clothes
Born in Bethlehem	None of His bones would be broken
Called Emmanuel	He would be buried in a rich man's tomb
Would Enter Jerusalem on a Donkey	He would rise from the dead

Prophecies Concerning World Events

The prophet Daniel accurately prophesied the rise of consecutive world empires. Writing during the reign of the Babylonian king Nebuchadnezzar, he described in detail on three different occasions the coming world rulers. First the Kingdom of Persia (the Medes and Persians) followed by the Kingdom of Greece. He described in specific detail the speed at which Alexander the Great would conquer the world and the brevity of his young life. He went on to describe the division of Greece under four different leaders. Later he told of the rule of Antiochus Epiphanies and the Maccabean revolt.

He then accurately described the coming of the Roman Empire with all its power and ferocity. He concluded with a prophecy concerning a kingdom which would contain aspects of the Roman Empire and be destroyed by God's final rule and Kingdom.[61] In addition, Daniel wrote that a Persian king would issue a decree to rebuild the city of Jerusalem and that 483 years

---

61 Daniel 2:1-45 / 7:1-8 & 8:1-27 NIV

later the Messiah would be killed (cut off). Following the issuance of this decree by Artaxerxes to Nehemiah in 444 BC,[62] Jesus was crucified 483 years later.[63]

The Apostle John continues Daniel's prophecy by telling us that there were two kingdoms before Babylon—Egypt and Assyria—and that a seventh and eighth kingdom would come to power. The seventh was most likely Germany under Adolph Hitler. The eighth has not yet come.[64]

Many other prophecies describe coming events. One cannot know so many details of the future without being connected to an eternal creator who exists outside of time and space. Any human that speaks clearly and consistently about the future can only receive that information from the Creator. Psychics and prophets may tell you about your past. However, knowledge of those events could have been gathered from other sources, so they cannot be that reliable. Intimate, accurate knowledge of the future comes only from the Creator and is strong evidence that the Bible is the Creator's message to mankind.

---

62   McDowell, Josh. The New Evidence That Demands A Verdict (Thomas Nelson Publishers, Nashville, Tennessee, 1999)
63   Daniel 9:24-27
64   Revelation 17:3-10.

Chapter Seven

Theodicy: When God Doesn't Answer Prayer

By his own admission, Bart Ehrman, author of *How Jesus Became God,* abandoned his faith in part over his understanding of God's lack of response to human suffering. Theodicy is rooted in the statement, "Why does an all-powerful God allow evil in the world?" During a debate with Dinesh D'Souza, *Ehrman remarked that there was no good answer to this dilemma.* He eventually became an agnostic and rejected the God of the Bible, a God who claims to intervene with humanity.[65]

A God of Order

When Dr. Michio Kaku acknowledged the existence of an intelligent creator, it represented a significant change in the conversation between theism and atheism, creationists and mainline scientists. A slim majority of scientists believe in God or some higher power, but it is unusual for well-known scientists to make public statements that support theism.

Acknowledging the existence of a creator, specifically a god of order, is no different than acknowledging the creationist argument of intelligent design, an argument that atheistic evolutionists have mocked for many decades. Dr. Kaku's words are significant:

> *"I have concluded that we are in a world made by rules created by an intelligence. To me, it is clear that we exist in a plan which is governed by rules that were created, shaped by a universal intelligence and not by chance. Personally, I think there's much wisdom in the god of Einstein.*

Dr. Kaku also said:

> *"There are two gods. One god is a personal god, the god that you pray to, the god that smites the Philistines, the god that walks on water. That's the first God, but there's another god, and that's the god of Spinoza. That's the god of beauty, harmony, simplicity."*[66]

Albert Einstein, Spinoza, Dr. Kaku and others believe there is a god of order and beauty, but they reject the God of the Bible. They don't understand how a noble God could allow evil in the world. Astrophysicist Neil deGrasse Tyson asks why a good God wouldn't stop or intervene in the myriads of ways the earth destroys human beings—death and destruction due to tornadoes, hurricanes, earthquakes, droughts, floods and mudslides.[67]

____

66 (bigthink.com/culture-religion
67 YouTube video with Dr. Tyson- www.youtube.com/

 Bridging the Origins Divide

Often it seems what is needed in one place is overdone in another, such as flooding in Mississippi but drought in the West. It's reasonable to ask why an all-powerful creator wouldn't send rain to dry areas and stop torrential rain in others. Is God good or evil? The philosopher Epicurus said it well:

"Either God wants to abolish evil, and cannot; or he can, but does not want to; or he cannot and does not want to. If he wants to, but cannot, he is impotent. If he can, and does not want to, he is wicked. But, if God both can and wants to abolish evil, then how comes evil in the world?"[68]

Why does a good and all-powerful god allow evil and suffering in the world? Why on occasion does he allow bad things to happen to good people? It would seem Earth is not so great and has many operational flaws. The Greeks dealt with this dilemma by imagining multiple gods, some good and some evil, who battled for control of the universe.

According to the Bible, the original Earth was perfect. It was without death, disease, murder or hatred, and there was no evil. There were no storms or rain, as the earth was watered by mist and underground streams. With no tornadoes, earthquakes or natural disasters, Adam and Eve truly lived in paradise. The long-term plan and purpose of the Creator was to create people who could know, love and understand who He was without coercion. This was free will.

The Consequences of Human Behavior

We fail to recognize the severity of our choices and the effects they have on our lives and the physical world. Most of the suffering in the world comes from human beings. Think of all the

---

68   Epicurus (341-270 BC) 2000 Years of Disbelief

suffering caused by theft, assault, fraud, murder, rape and sexual abuse. From a moral perspective there is adultery, lying, betrayal, jealousy, meanness, mocking and hatred. These are all due to human behavior.

Seemingly random events can result in a series of disastrous consequences. For example, the abusive childhood Charles Manson experienced most assuredly contributed to the deaths at the Tate La Bianca homes and altered the trajectory of the hippie movement. Peace and love lost their influence after those murders along with the chaos of Woodstock.

If every human obeyed the Ten Commandments, about 90% of suffering would end. The world would be a much better place. The introduction of sin into the world changed everything. Sin is like a computer virus. It begins as a simple issue; but left unchecked, it will eventually corrupt and destroy its host.

Why did the Creator give us this power? Perhaps it was His only choice. He must allow us to choose. If He wants to be known and loved by His creations, he must allow mankind to obey or disobey without force. The choices we make must be ours, even if our decisions cause us or others harm.

The natural world is governed by its own laws. Spiritual and metaphysical laws are just as real and immutable as natural law. These laws interact with and affect our personal lives and our relationship with the planet. Sowing, reaping, blessing and cursing have both positive and negative effects on our lives.

Sin has very religious overtones and is not a topic most people want to discuss. It is often considered anti-fun and uncool. However, sin is living outside God's order and structure. Sin is like pouring soda onto your motherboard; nothing is going

   Bridging the Origins Divide

to work properly after doing so. Because of sin there is much suffering in the world. The choices God gave us were significant and have significant consequences.

God's laws are for us. They protect us from ourselves and our self-destructive behavior. God is not against sexual activity, but He understands the power it has over human behavior. Intercourse outside of marriage and a committed relationship is deeply destructive. It has been responsible for broken marriages, damaged children and grandchildren, child abuse, unwanted and unloved children, and even wars and murder. God's rules are not evil or harmful. Again, human disobedience and rebellion have caused most of the suffering the world has known.

The Role of Bloodshed

Death is the ultimate penalty for bad human choices. There is a relationship between innocent bloodshed and the catastrophic events that kill so many each year. It is not one-to-one, though. If someone dies in an earthquake, it does not mean their personal sin or rebellion was the cause; rather, it is collective. When these catastrophes occur, we are all affected. It is a statement to humans that we are vulnerable to the effects of sin. Instead of calling out to the Creator and turning from our disobedience, we curse him and blame him for his inaction.

The Creator values human life.

"If someone is found slain, lying in a field in the land the Lord your God is giving you to possess, and it is not known who the killer was, your elders and judges shall go out and measure the distance from the body to the neighboring towns. Then the elders of the town nearest

*the body shall take a heifer that has never been worked
and has never worn a yoke and lead it down to a valley
that has not been plowed or planted and where there is
a flowing stream. There in the valley they are to break
the heifer's neck. The Levitical priests shall step forward,
for the Lord your God has chosen them to minister and
to pronounce blessings in the name of the Lord and to
decide all cases of dispute and assault. Then all the elders
of the town nearest the body shall wash their hands over
the heifer whose neck was broken in the valley, and they
shall declare: "Our hands did not shed this blood, nor did
our eyes see it done. Accept this atonement for your people Israel, whom you have redeemed, Lord, and do not
hold your people guilty of the blood of an innocent person." Then the bloodshed will be atoned for, and you will
have purged from yourselves the guilt of shedding innocent blood, since you have done what is right in the eyes
of the Lord.*

—Deuteronomy 21:1-9

The sixth commandment, "You shall not kill," shows us that
the shedding of innocent human blood has always been a great
concern to the Creator.

In this passage, the creator is deeply interested in the death of
a stranger, a person unknown to those living in the area. Though
people nearby had no connection to him, they were required to
sacrifice something of great value to atone for his death. In this
case they were required to sacrifice a special heifer. This was
done to cleanse the land of the pollution from the bloodshed.

*"Do not pollute the land where you are. Bloodshed pol-
lutes the land, and atonement cannot be made for the*

                                   Bridging the Origins Divide

—Numbers 35:33

In that world, a heifer was of great value. The sacrifice they were required to make was a temporary solution to the death of a stranger. Ultimately God will judge the murderer. Until that time, the land must be cleansed by a sacrifice that covers the sin. Human life is of infinite worth, enough for the Creator to lay down His life for ours.

> *"For the creation was subjected to futility, not willingly, but because of Him who subjected it, in hope that the creation itself also will be set free from its slavery to corruption into the freedom of the glory of the children of God. For we know that the whole creation groans and suffers the pains of childbirth together until now."*

—Romans 8:20-22

Earthquakes, famine, volcanoes, hurricanes, tornadoes and other natural disasters are due in part to the consequences of violence and bloodshed upon the land. Apart from the death of Jesus as the atonement for mankind's sin, they earth may very well have destroyed itself many years ago.

Rather than call out to the Creator to ask forgiveness for senseless bloodshed, we blame and cry out against Him when disasters occur, demanding He be accountable for these disasters. The Creator will respond with forgiveness and healing, but we must come back to Him and turn from our rebellion against His ways. We must pray for the healing of the earth and ask forgiveness for the bloodshed that has taken place over the centuries at the hands of human beings.

Shared Authority

We are confusing the Creator's omnipotence with a willingness to control everything. To safeguard against bad events, the Creator would need complete control of our actions. Human beings would be like robots with no free will under the control of the Creator. However, if we have a voice in our actions, then the Creator has limited His own power to control good and evil. In essence He has shared His control of the universe with us.

This is precisely what the Bible teaches. The Creator is all powerful, but he does not control all things. The Creator told us to pray, "Thy Kingdom come, thy will be done on earth as it is in heaven." He has allotted control of the planet and universe in part to human beings. We are individuals who can choose to recognize and interact with the Creator. Ask any teacher, preacher, warden, boss or parent of a two-year-old, and you will find they are in resolute agreement with the willfulness of human beings.

Noah's flood destroyed God's perfect world.

Sin and bad human choices led to the destruction of God's perfect world. Why would an all-powerful Creator make a world with so many flaws? Why wouldn't He anticipate the destructive forces of nature and find ways to avoid them?

According to the Bible, a global flood destroyed the perfect world God created, leaving us with a beautiful but flawed earth. The earth's mantle fractured, and the land mass of Pangea separated. There were 40 days and 40 nights of heavy rainfall, and floods covered the entire earth for over 150 days. Earth's geology and atmosphere changed radically. Today, our world is plagued with volcanoes, tornadoes, earthquakes, hurricanes, tsunamis and other natural disasters.

*"The Lord saw how great the wickedness of the human
race had become on the earth, and that every inclina-
tion of the thoughts of the human heart was only evil all
the time. The Lord regretted that he had made human
beings on the earth, and his heart was deeply troubled. So
the Lord said, "I will wipe from the face of the earth the
human race I have created—and with them the animals,
the birds and the creatures that move along the ground—
for I regret that I have made them."*

—Genesis 6:5-8

*"Now the earth was corrupt in God's sight and was full
of violence. God saw how corrupt the earth had become,
for all the people on earth had corrupted their ways. So,
God said to Noah, "I am going to put an end to all people,
for the earth is filled with violence because of them. I am
surely going to destroy both them and the earth. So, make
yourself an ark of cypress wood; make rooms in it and
coat it with pitch inside and out."*

—Genesis 6:11-14

Was Noah's flood a global event?

World-renowned underwater archaeologist, Robert Ballard,
believes he has found proof that the biblical flood was based on
real events. While Ballard does not say this was Noah's global
flood, he has found evidence of a massive flood that buried
entire populations over four hundred feet below the present
landmass.

*"We went in there to look for the flood [...] Four hun-
dred feet below the surface, they unearthed an ancient
shoreline, proof to Ballard that a catastrophic event did*

This is only one of many places around the globe that appear to be deeply affected by a massive flood. There are numerous locations around the earth that display similar characteristics, such as the Channeled Scablands in eastern Washington, Greenland's Grand Canyon, Mount Saint Helens Canyons, and the US Grand Canyon

The entire earth looks like what we see in the Grand Canyon. Not all canyons have the same exact layers, but the surface of the earth covers a massive graveyard of human, animal and floral life destroyed in the global flood. Lakes are often formed in the aftermath of massive volcanic activity. Larger lakes sometimes form natural dams around them. When those break, tons of water flood outward under tremendous pressure and carve out the types of canyons we see today.

There are two opposing worldviews regarding a global flood—an old earth evolutionary one and a more literal "young earth" one based on creationism. As a theologian and Bible teacher, I will stand with the biblical record and scientists who objectively evaluate the data we have. Of course, no one witnessed the flood, and no one can explain every aspect of its effect on the earth's geology.

Which worldview best explains the evidence we see and fits within a biblical paradigm? We tend to interpret facts through

---

69   abcnews.go.com

                                              Bridging the Origins Divide

assumptions. A good example is plate tectonics. Old earth science believes the process of subduction (one continent slipping under another) is the cause for the high mountains on the earth and fossilized sea creatures found on the tops of those mountains. Young earth creationists believe that same basic idea, but the scientists say it took millions of years to form the mountains. Creation scientists believe it was rapid. The earthquakes and volcanoes we see are the result of the Great Flood. After 4,500 years, the earth is still not fully stable and continues to experience aftershocks.

Biblical Arguments for a Global Flood

What happened (the story):

"In the six hundredth year of Noah's life, on the seventeenth day of the second month—on that day all the springs of the great deep burst forth, and the floodgates of the heavens were opened. And rain fell on the earth forty days and forty nights [...] For forty days the flood kept coming on the earth, and as the waters increased, they lifted the ark high above the earth. The waters rose and increased greatly on the earth, and the ark floated on the surface of the water.

"They rose greatly on the earth, and all the high mountains under the entire heavens were covered. The waters rose and covered the mountains to a depth of more than fifteen cubits. Every living thing that moved on land perished—birds, livestock, wild animals, all the creatures that swarm over the earth, and all mankind. Everything on dry land that had the breath of life in its nostrils died. Every living thing on the face of the earth was wiped out;

people and animals and the creatures that moved along the ground and the birds were wiped from the earth. Only Noah was left, and those with him in the ark.

—Genesis 7:11-24

The Length of the Flood.

"The springs of the great deep opened and the floodgates of heaven opened. The rain fell for 40 days and 40 nights." This was not a broken dam or an overflowing river. The earth was flooded for 150 days. Local floods do not last that long. Additionally, it was 7 more months before the waters had drained off the surface of the earth. During all this time the volcanoes and water erosion were changing and forming the earth we see today. All the mountains of the earth were covered with water.

The original mountains were perhaps 2,000–3,000 feet high. Today, we see fossilized skeletons of sea creatures on the tops of the highest mountains. Remnants of ancient sea life have been found fossilized on Everest, the world's highest point above sea level. These include fragments of extinct and existing marine animals including trilobites, ostracods and crinoids.

God said he would destroy every living creature he had made.

"Seven days from now I will send rain on the earth for forty days and forty nights, and I will wipe from the face of the earth every living creature I have made."

—Genesis 7:4

A local flood would not destroy every living thing on the earth. God promised to never destroy the earth again with a flood.

"Never again will all life be destroyed by the waters of

Bridging the Origins Divide

a flood; never again will there be a flood to destroy the earth.”

—Genesis 9:11.

Jesus spoke of the flood in the New Testament.

"As it was in the days of Noah, so it will be at the coming of the Son of Man. For in the days before the flood, people were eating and drinking, marrying and giving in marriage, up to the day Noah entered the ark; and they knew nothing about what would happen until the flood came and took them all away."

—Matthew 24:37-39

Why would you need to build an ark? Why take two of every animal if it was just a local flood? In a local flood the animals could migrate to higher land away from the flooded area and they would not all die.

Local floods commonly take place around the world. If the Flood was local, then God's promise was a lie.

The separation of Pangea was caused by a major catastrophic event.

"Go into the ark, you and your whole family, because I have found you righteous in this generation. Take with you seven pairs of every kind of clean animal, a male and its mate, and one pair of every kind of unclean animal, a male and its mate, and seven pairs of every kind of bird, male and female, to keep their various kinds alive throughout the earth.

—Genesis 7:1-3

Jesus confirmed flood and the extent of the damage.

"As it was in the days of Noah, so it will be at the coming

of the Son of Man. 38 For in the days before the flood,
people were eating and drinking, marrying and giving in
marriage, up to the day Noah entered the ark; 39 and
they knew nothing about what would happen until the
flood came and took them all away."

—Matthew 24:37-39

Peter confirmed the flood and the extent of the damage.

"…through which the world at that time was destroyed by
being flooded with water."

—2 Peter 3:6

The reason for the flood was the wickedness of humanity. How does that work with a local flood explanation? Are we saying that only the people in that area were wicked, and the rest of the earth was not?

How would you contain a local flood? If the high mountains were created during and after the flood, they would not be high enough to act as boundaries to hold the waters. They would have flowed over the whole of Pangea.

280 cultures have a flood story. The stories are different, but there are enough similarities to make an argument for a worldwide flood.

The Breaking of the Pangea

To break apart continents would require forces beyond our comprehension.

"In the six hundredth year of Noah's life, on the seven-
teenth day of the second month—on that day all the
springs of the great deep burst forth, and the floodgates of

the heavens were opened. And rain fell on the earth forty days and forty nights."

—Genesis 7:11-12

Literally, it says the springs of the vast abyss broke forth. It was wrenched open, and the crevices of the heavens were opened. This was more than just water. It was the breaking apart of the earth's mantle on the ocean floor. Massive volcanic eruptions created the high mountains and deep valleys we see today.

This same rendering of the ocean floors would have split the continents apart and caused rapid separation, producing massive tsunamis across the globe.

Old earth scientists assume today's continental drift is between 1.5 centimeters (0.6 inches per year[70] and has been the same throughout history and that it took hundreds of millions of years for the continents to drift apart.

What if we are seeing today the last movements of the rapid separation which began with the initial breaking of the continents during the Flood? For example, if I pushed a man on roller skates from one end of the rink toward the other and used only one push, the speed of his movement would have almost completely stopped by the time he reached the other end. This is analogous to the moving continents.

Marine Fossils on Mountains Around the Earth

We find many hundreds of marine fossils on almost every high mountain, including Mt. Everest. Most are buried in sedimentary rocks on the continents. Ocean waters had to totally flood the continents. They had to flood the continents when the mountains were lower than they are

---

70   www.google.com/search?q=how+fast+are+the+continents+moving+today

today. Which argues for a rapid rise of the earth's mountain ranges, and a rapid deposition of the sedimentary layers on the mountains. Of course, scientists who have outright rejected Noah's flood have a different explanation for fossils in the high mountains, however, their story is no better than the Creation story, which in fact gives a better more complete argument for the geology of the earth.[71]

Massive Fossil Graveyards Around the World

Countless billions of plants and animal fossils are found buried in extensive graveyards around the world. One fossil graveyard stretches for 180 miles (290 km) across northern Arizona and into southern Nevada, covering an area of at least 10,500 square miles (30,000 km2). "in another fossil graveyard in Montceau-les-Mines, France, hundreds of thousands of marine creatures were buried with amphibians, spiders, scorpions, millipedes, insects, and reptiles. These marine and land-dwelling creatures are found buried together on the continent. How could this have happened unless the ocean waters rose and rapidly swept over the continents in the catastrophic global flood?[72]

Because many fish were buried alive, the fine details of their fins and eye sockets have been preserved.

Even the compound lenses in many trilobite eyes are still available for detailed study. Some squids were fossilized with ink still in their ink sacs. And in a classic example of rapid burial, an ichthyosaur (marine reptile) about 6

---

71   answersingenesis.org/the- flood/global/evidences- genesis-flood/
72   IBID

                              Bridging the Origins Divide

feet (2 meters) long was fossilized at the moment of giving birth. One minute this huge creature had just delivered her baby, then seconds later, without time to escape, mother and baby were entombed in a catastrophic avalanche of lime mud.[73]

Sediment Spreading Across Continents

Covering vast areas on every continent are sedimentary rock layers laid down by the catastrophic flood conditions. Many of these sediment layers can be traced all the way across continents and even between continents. For example, the Cretaceous chalk beds of southern England, well known as spectacular white cliffs along the coast, can be traced west and north across England and appear again in Northern Ireland. In the opposite direction, these same chalk beds can be traced across France, the Netherlands, Germany, Poland, southern Scandinavia, and other parts of Europe to Turkey, then to Israel and Egypt and as far as Kazakhstan. Remarkably, the same chalk beds with the same fossils and the same distinctive strata (layers) above and below them are also found in the Midwest USA, from Nebraska to Texas, and from Alabama and Arkansas to Colorado. They also appear in the Perth Basin of Western Australia.[74]

Features of the Sedimentary Layers

It is hard to imagine what forces were necessary to deposit such a vast, continent-wide series of layers. But some of

---

73   IBID
74   IBID

the features in the layers give us a good indication of that force. For example, there are huge boulders at the bottom of the Tapeats Sandstone, and the unit consists of beds of sand eroded from the underlying, hard crystalline rocks and deposited by violent storms. This is evidence that massive forces deposited these sediment layers rapidly and violently across the entire USA and beyond across North Africa and the Middle East. Today's slow- and-gradual processes cannot account for this catastrophic deposition, but the global flood cataclysm can.[75]

No Sign of Millions of Years Between the Layers

If the sedimentary layers took hundreds of millions of years to accumulate at today's slow rates, then the boundaries between many sedimentary strata should be broken by lots of topographic relief with weathered surfaces from millions of years of wear and erosion after each layer was deposited. However, under the catastrophic conditions of the cataclysmic global flood, even if land surfaces were briefly exposed, any erosion would have been rapid and widespread, generally leaving behind flat and smooth surfaces.[76]

Evidence in the Folds

Further evidence that these layers were laid down quickly, not over millions of years, are the folds we find in these sediment layers. When hard rock is bent (or folded), it invariably fractures and breaks because it is

---

75 IBID
76 IBID

   Bridging the Origins Divide

brittle. Only unhardened rock can bend when it is soft and pliable (plastic) like modeling clay. When water deposits sediments in a layer, some water is left behind, trapped between the sediment grains. As other sedimentary layers are laid on top of them, the pressure squeezes the sediment grains closer together and forces out much of the water. As the sediment layer dries out, the chemicals that were in the water between the grains convert into a natural cement. This cement transforms the originally soft and wet sediment layer into hard, brittle rock. This process can occur within hours but generally takes days or months, depending on the prevailing conditions. However, it doesn't take millions of years.[77]

Other Resources.[78]

Charles Lyell claimed to have *"freed a significant number of church leaders from Moses*[79], referring to leaders who have accepted his lies as truth and consider Genesis 1-11 as mythological.

Evidence for a global flood is overwhelming and demonstrates the reliability of the biblical record, yet many church leaders will not teach or discuss biblical creationism, the Flood, the Fall and other significant topics in the Genesis record. These are considered divisive and unpopular topics, that often create conflict. My hope and prayers are that you will seriously consider or reconsider the evidence and what it means for biblical Christianity.

The Apostle Peter told us that the Flood is a warning for the

---

77   IBID

78   Dr. Andrew Snelling "What is the Geological Evidence for a Young Earth?" www.youtube.com/watch?v=Q9yc3BdeSds&t=4s The evidence of Catastrophic Plate Tectonics

79   answersingenesis.org/the- flood/global/evidences- genesis-flood

world today, a reminder that there will be a final judgment on humanity in the days to come.

> *"But do not forget this one thing, dear friends: With the Lord a day is like a thousand years, and a thousand years are like a day. The Lord is not slow in keeping his promise, as some understand slowness. Instead, he is patient with you, not wanting anyone to perish, but everyone to come to repentance. But the day of the Lord will come like a thief. The heavens will disappear with a roar; the elements will be destroyed by fire, and the earth and everything done in it will be laid bare.*

> *"Since everything will be destroyed in this way, what kind of people ought you to be? You ought to live holy and godly lives as you look forward to the day of God and speed its coming. That day will bring about the destruction of the heavens by fire, and the elements will melt in the heat. But in keeping with his promise we are looking forward to a new heaven and a new earth, where righteousness dwells. So then, dear friends, since you are looking forward to this, make every effort to be found spotless, blameless and at peace with him."*

> —2 Peter 3:8-14

Chapter Eight

How Were the Heavens and Earth Created?

The Biblical Record of Creation

From a strictly human point of view, it is impossible to know the exact process God used to create the universe. No one except the Creator was there as a witness. God could have used any process He wanted and taken as long as He wished.

We have mentioned that natural selection and the big bang are not the causes for the universe. If God used either of those processes, it would still indicate He is an eternal, intelligent and powerful entity. The need for meaning, morality and accountability would remain the same.

The reputation and authority of the Bible are on the line. If the Bible is the Creator's message to mankind, then its account of creation is accurate. As the ultimate author of the Bible, God has declared He created the earth a certain way and in a specific time frame, so why would we doubt it? Why should we seek a natural explanation when the biblical definition is clear and precise?

Ultimately, supernatural creation makes sense if there is a Creator. Evolution appears to make sense only when you attempt to explain the universe apart from a Creator. Since evolution cannot explain causation, it is at best an incomplete theory. The modern views of science and evolution are conflicted and need to be resolved.

The Genesis Account of Creation

The Genesis record of Creation is the only written history of the universe from its inception through the first century AD. Genesis 1 and 2 are the only non-mythical accounts of creation that can be seriously considered as history *(see Appendix 3)*.

The Genesis record gives us almost 6,000 years of human history. The Bible tells us the Creator made the universe in six consecutive days. He created the earth, sun, moon, stars, trees and vegetation. He created all living creatures from the spider to the great dinosaurs, ending with his crowning achievement: human beings.

The Bible declares that God created a perfect world without problems such as natural disasters, sickness or disease. When God finished His activity, He declared everything was good. This indicates a creation with none of the problems we face in today's world.

God made mankind as both a physical and spiritual being. The spiritual part of us, which He called the soul, is eternal and part of His own nature. The physical part is of course our bodies.

God gave us authority over all of creation. Plants, animals and the earth are ours to care for and use as we see fit. Along with this authority, He gave us parameters concerning the care and stewardship of His earth and creatures.

 Bridging the Origins Divide

The first eleven chapters of Genesis cover approximately 2,000 years of mankind's history. They give a detailed account of mankind's rejection of the Creator's instructions and how that rejection ultimately led to a worldwide flood and the death and destruction of most humans living at that time. It tells us that the Flood was global and declares it as one of the primary causes for the present geology of Earth.

The Scriptures declare that God made the universe in six solar days.

> *"For in six days the Lord made the heavens and the earth and all that is in them, and rested on the seventh day, therefore the Lord blessed the Sabbath day and made it holy".*
>
> —Exodus 20:11

> *"You shall keep the Sabbath, because it is holy for you. Everyone who profanes it shall be put to death. Whoever does any work on it, that soul shall be cut off from among his people. Six days shall work be done, but the seventh day is a Sabbath of solemn rest, holy to the Lord. Whoever does any work on the Sabbath day shall be put to death. Therefore, the people of Israel shall keep the Sabbath, observing the Sabbath throughout their generations, as a covenant forever. It is a sign forever between me and the people of Israel that in six days the Lord made heaven and earth, and on the seventh day he rested and was refreshed."*
>
> —Exodus 31:14-17

Jesus confirmed a young earth by declaring that Adam was there from the beginning of Creation. If you add our modern reckoning of time to the Genesis record, it means Adam was billions of years old. The heavens and earth could not have been created billions of years before Adam.

"He answered, "Have you not read that he who created them from the beginning made them male and female."

—Matthew 19:4

"But from the beginning of creation, God made them male and female."

—Mark 10:6

The six 24-hour days of creation demonstrate a direct chronology from the sixth day of creation to the time of Abraham, approximately 2,000 years later.

"In the beginning God created the heavens and the earth. Now the earth was formless and empty, darkness was over the surface of the deep, and the Spirit of God was hovering over the waters. And God said, "Let there be light," and there was light. God saw that the light was good, and he separated the light from the darkness. God called the light "day," and the darkness he called "night." And there was evening, and there was morning, the first day.

—Genesis 1:1-5

This pattern is repeated five more times. Each day, as a portion of our world is created, the narrative closes with the phrase, "and there was evening, and there was morning, the second day, third day…" On the seventh day, God rests (stops) His creative activity and more importantly declares the universe was fully ordered without flaw.

In Chapter 5, Moses gives us the genealogy of Adam and

Bridging the Origins Divide

his direct descendants. Verses 1 through 5 show us the pattern for this record.

> *"This is the book of the generations of Adam. When God created man, he made him in the likeness of God. Male and female he created them, and he blessed them and named them Man when they were created. When Adam had lived 130 years, he fathered a son in his own likeness, after his image, and named him Seth. The days of Adam after he fathered Seth were 800 years; and he had other sons and daughters. When Adam lived 130 years, he had a son in his own likeness, in his own image; and he named him Seth. After Seth was born, Adam lived 800 years and had other sons and daughters. Altogether, Adam lived 930 years, and then he died."*
>
> —Genesis 5:1-5

The age of the first-born is then given, and the age of his death follows. The period between Adam and Noah (the Flood) is 1,650 years. Abraham was born almost 400 years after Noah. Thus, the biblical timeline covers approximately 2,000 years from the creation of Adam until Abraham.

Genesis 12 through Malachi chapter 4 covers the next 1,600 years of history. The last book of the Old Testament, Malachi, was written approximately 400 years before Christ's birth. So, it was approximately 2,000 years from Abraham to Christ, and 2,000 years from Christ to today.

Thus, the Bible teaches that man's history from creation to today is approximately 6,000 years. Is the timeline complete? Some who believe in a young earth add another 4,000 years to earth's history, giving us a possible time span of 6,000-10,000 years.[80] That may seem quite young compared to the billions of years of evolution, but this timeline fits quite well with the "known" history of mankind, which is approximately 10,000 years based on the dating of certain objects.

There are problems with the dating of historical items using Carbon-14 techniques. Carbon-14 has a short life span of approximately 5,730 years. Significant changes in the level of Carbon-12 in the atmosphere could dramatically affect the dating of things before the global flood. This would explain some of the older carbon-14 dates falling within the 10,000-20,000-year range.

Answering the Critics

For the past 500 years, theologians and Bible scholars have developed a variety of ways to interpret Genesis 1 to avoid contradicting the long ages of geological time proposed by modern science. Most if not all these theories were developed around the time that geology began proposing long ages of time for the earth. The gap theory and theistic evolution were proposed publicly by Thomas Chalmers around 1814 and 1877 respectively. Theistic evolution was proposed by John W Dawson in 1877.

Other theories include the day age theory, progressive creationism and the allegorical theory. Also of note are "The Bible is just wrong" and "The Bible is not a book of science, so what it says about science does not matter." Some say the first day did not occur until day four when the sun was created. A recent interpretation argues that the Genesis record was not about the creation of matter but only focused on bringing order out of chaos. This should not be confused with the scientific chaos theory.

These theories incorporate long ages of time and ask us to

---

80   www.setterfield.org/000docs/homecopy.htm

                                    Bridging the Origins Divide

ignore textual details favoring creation. Were there not a controversy over the age of the earth, most of those theories would not be relevant, much less argued with such virulence.

Questions about the Genesis record are not new. Augustine spoke on literal interpretation based on "light before luminaries" (illumination before sun and stars). He also was not sure about the 7th day, was it 24 hours or an age of time. The point is that the age of the earth is has much more significance today than before it was an "absolute doctrine of" evolutionary science.

Are the days in Genesis 24 hours long?

Is it possible the Genesis account has been misunderstood? If the six days of creation are not literal, it might be possible to correspond them with long ages as reckoned by science. There are significant problems with interpreting the Genesis account as non-literal, though. Let's address some of the more popular arguments against a literal six-day creation week.

The Genesis account is the story of creation and is to be taken figuratively.

Many Christian leaders believe the Genesis account is not to be taken literally and that it is a story of creation. The language of the text is viewed as symbolic or poetic. Several factors must be considered on this point.

Is the language poetic? A detailed analysis of narrative and poetic literature in the Old Testament demonstrated that Genesis Chapter One is narrative and not poetic. Research done by the RATE team, a group of eight accredited young earth creation scientists, examined the dating techniques and other teachings of conventional science. They discovered serious issues with the old earth belief system. Their findings were presented in the book, *Thousands Not Billions*. One study compared types of verbs used in narrative writing against poetic usage. For example, the crossing of the Red Sea is told in two different stories. Genesis 14 is the narrative account, and Genesis 15 is the poetic version known as the *Song of Moses*. Approximately 522 texts were studied; 295 were narrative and 227 were poetic. Narrative prose is consistently different from poetic throughout the entire Old Testament. Genesis 1:1–2:3 was compared to the poetic Psalm 104 accounting of creation. The pattern shows Genesis 1 is narrative.[81]

Furthermore, the verifiable scientific facts in the passage are all true: There are at least four reasons to believe the days in Genesis are literally twenty-four hours long.

1. Everything reproduces after its own kind. As far as anyone can observe, all plants and animals reproduce after their own kind. Giraffes cannot mate with the hippopotamus or elephants with mice. The biblical definition of "kind" is any animal or plant that can reproduce. If they cannot reproduce, or if their offspring cannot continue to reproduce, they are not the same kind.

2. Humans and animals were vegetarian. God originally created all animals and human beings as vegetarians. It was after the Flood when God gave us permission to kill and eat animals. As a result, they became fearful of mankind. In the Book of Isaiah, it forecasts that the lion will once again lie down with the lamb and that a child will play with a poisonous snake.

3. The purpose for the sun, moon and stars as stated in Genesis 1 is accurate. God said He made a lesser light to rule the night and a greater light to rule the day. The stars are also

---

81   DeYoung, Dr. Donald. Thousands Not Billions, Master Books, August 2005.

                                   Bridging the Origins Divide

used as signs for the seasons, and sailors once navigated the open seas by following the stars.

4. The seven days of creation established a pattern for mankind. Genesis 1:1-5 defines a day as 24 hours with half daylight and half-darkness.

Why did God take six days when He could have made it in one? It was to establish the seven-day week and the annual cycles of life. The seven days of creation and a 24-hour day are the established pattern for all human existence. From Abraham through today, everyone has used a seven-day week. The Babylonians, Persians and Romans all used the seven-day week before the advent of Christianity.[82] A seven-day week is used in all societies and most likely dates to the days of Adam.

The 24-hour model has a different order of events from the scientific model.

There are important differences between the theory of evolution and the biblical account. For example, science says the stars were created first. The Bible says they were created on day four after the earth, which was created on day one.

Science claims the earth came into existence out of molten rock and fire that resulted from the death of a star 4.5 billion years ago. Genesis says God created the earth out of water.

> *"Then God said, 'Let the waters below the heavens be gathered into one place, and let the dry land appear.' [...] God called the dry land "Earth."*

> —Genesis 1:3-11

The apostle Peter confirms this:

> *"But they deliberately forget that long ago by God's word,*

---

82 webexhibits.org/calendars/week.html

*the heavens existed, and the earth was formed out of
water and by water."*

—2 Peter 3:4-7

A six-day creation exalts the power and majesty of the Creator.

Exodus 20:11 tells us the basis for worship of God is because He created everything in six days out of nothing. We worship an all-powerful Creator who has occasionally intervened in an evolutionary process.

> *"In six days, the LORD made the heavens and the earth, the sea, and all that is in them, but he rested on the seventh day. Therefore, the LORD blessed the Sabbath day and made it holy."*

—Exodus 20:11

Could it all have happened over six twenty-four-hour days?
Perhaps the most persuasive argument from a biblical, old earth perspective is that there is not enough time to do all God said He did on a given day. It has been pointed out that on days three and six there was not enough time for God to accomplish everything in 24 hours. Concerning day three:

An Accelerated Natural Process

One possible solution to a six-day creation is that God created everything using an accelerated natural process. He would have created the universe using natural laws but at an accelerated pace. The normal time it takes for a tree to grow from seed to fruit would have taken place in a single day rather than 10 to 50 years or so.

If the initial creation of everything took place at an accelerated speed, the universe would appear to be many thousands or

Bridging the Origins Divide

even millions of years old, but it could appear to be between six and ten thousand years old as we observe today.

An accelerated natural process would also affect the apparent age of the earth. The creation of the earth would have been finished in a single day. Each subsequent day's events would have been completed in a single day as well—plants, stars, animals and humans.

All the laws of creation would have been in operation but at a faster speed. The creation of rocks and heavy elements would have been accelerated. If everything were naturally accelerated, living things would reach their maturity quicker.

Any examination of the universe one day after the creation would have shown all the outward signs of long age despite being quite young. This would be like watching a movie in fast forward mode. The entire movie is there; it is just going by quicker because you pushed that speed button. God may have accelerated the entire natural process, then slowed it down to normal speed when He was finished with creation.

Trees and Vegetation

Then God said, "Let the land produce vegetation: seed-bearing plants and trees on the land that bear fruit with seed in it, according to their various kinds. And it was so. The land produced vegetation: plants bearing seed according to their kinds and trees bearing fruit with seed in them, according to their kinds. And God saw that it was good. And there was evening, and there was morning—the third day."

The text implies a natural accelerated process; the trees grew and had fruit on them by the end of day three. So, in this 24-hour period, they not only grew to maturity but provided fruit for Adam to eat.

Dendrochronology is the study of tree rings. If you cut down a tree and examine the stump, you will find distinct rings indicating the number of years the tree has been alive. Each ring represents about a year in the life of the tree. During spring, new cells develop and quickly grow to produce a light brown ring. In the summer, the growth slows down and produces a darker cell. Access to ground water affects the speed of growth, most of which occurs in the spring.

Would the tree, created on the first day of creation, have rings? If they are an absolute part of the aging process, they would be there. If they only exist because of ground water availability, they might not have existed or been visible.

All life forms would have been complete and functional. Here, the Creator simply created all living things at their functional age. It's the chicken or the egg conundrum. The chicken comes first because the egg needs the chicken to hatch it.

Was Adam created as an infant or an adult? As an infant, how would he survive? God could have supernaturally protected, nurtured and raised him, but it would have been completely unnecessary. If living things can be spoken into existence, they can certainly be created fully grown.

There are indications in the Bible that Adam was an adult. He was given the task of naming the animals and caring for the garden. There were serious consequences for willful disobedience concerning what to eat in the garden.

If Adam had a complete physical exam on day seven, he would have most likely looked 30 years old without the wear and tear of a 30-year-old male. There would be some physical characteristics of age, but the natural aging process would not have begun until after the Fall when life expectancy would have been diminished.

 Bridging the Origins Divide

In many ways, this scenario would be required for any creation, evolution or ex-nihilo. Everything in the universe is dependent on everything else. Life cannot exist without a proper environment, the right amount of heat, sunlight, soil and water. Plants can't grow, and animals and humans would not survive if all the proper elements were not there at the exact moment in time.

Recall the earlier argument about the possibility of living things surviving on their own. They could only survive if they came into existence at a developed age and in an environment conducive to survival.

If God can create everything out of nothing, then why not create it complete and matured? Author John Morris calls this a "functionally mature universe."[83] Perhaps it was accomplished through an accelerated natural process. The goodness of God and His love for mankind led Him to plan and prepare a complete functional home filled with good things, beauty and wonder.

In Genesis, Moses tells us God created light on day one, then the sun, moon and stars on day four. Since the light we see comes from the sun, it would have made more sense to create the sun before the light. Why would Moses change what we consider the normal order of creation unless that is what happened?

The light of verse three dispelled the darkness of verse two. God was creating day and night not based on the sun and moon but solely on light and darkness, which is the absence of light. Thus, there was only darkness until God created light.

When the sun, moon and stars were created on day four, it was specifically to separate the day from night and to mark

---

83   Morris, John. The Young Earth; Master Books, P.O. Box 727, Green Forest, AR 72638.
      pg. 70

sacred times, seasons, days and years. The side of the earth away from the sun would have been dark, which is the same for all planets. From our perspective, the sun and moon separate the day from night. When we include the stars, all three can be used for time and calendar keeping. Even if the sun was not created until day four, there was still night during the first three days. Moses describes them as evening and morning on the first Day, then day two, day three, etc.

On several occasions, the Bible says that God stretched out the heavens (fabric of space). Assume the earth is the approximate center of the universe and the stars were created around the earth. If God stretched the stars outwards in every direction from the earth into space, the closest star to us at the time would have been visible on the earth from the beginning of creation. The stretching process is not unlike our observations of receding (redshifted) celestial objects.

Is Genesis 2 a different creation account?

Some have argued that the Bible has two different accounts of creation, one in the first chapter and another in chapter two. They are not different stories; rather, each account was written with a different purpose in mind.

Chapter one is a timeline. Chapter two is a more creative account focused primarily on the creation of Adam and Eve. The focus of the story is Adam's realization that he was alone which led to the subsequent establishment of marriage. Adam was created first and given three responsibilities: take care of the earth, teach Eve about spiritual matters, and name all the animals. This established a hierarchy in the garden before the Fall.

It is implied that Adam named all the animals on the sixth

   Bridging the Origins Divide

day. There is no absolute reason to believe he named all the animals before the creation of Eve or even at the end of day six. It is quite possible that over the next few days or weeks, Adam finished the task he started on day six.

Another scenario demonstrates a need for Adam to have a partner. The process could have gone like this. Adam is naming the animals that God created earlier in the day. During this process, Adam begins to realize he is all alone. The animals have partners, but he does not. God then caused Adam to sleep and created Eve.

There is no reason to reject the clear teaching of solar days found in chapter one based on the ambiguity of chapter two. If you must choose between the two, it is a more consistent interpretation to support a 24-hour day.

In the final analysis, every Christian must come to grips with the reality that we will not be able to agree on everything with the evolutionists. We should always give the Bible the benefit of the doubt in questionable areas. Even Hugh Ross, a hardcore Old Earth apologist, believes in special creation for Adam and Eve[84]

Factoring in long ages to the biblical text solves some problems, but it creates others as well. Science is asking questions that cannot be answered about the age of the universe and how God created it. This creates confusion and doubt about the authority of the Bible.

Was the fourth day of creation the first 24-hour day?
One of the latest theories that rejects a six-day creation is that there could not have been a "day" until the sun was created on day four. The implication is that since the first three days were

---

84 www.reasons.org/about/staff/ross.shtml

of indeterminate length without a sun, it calls into question the meaning of "day" in the text.

> *"In the beginning, God created the heavens and the earth. Now the earth was formless and empty, darkness was over the surface of the deep, and the Spirit of God was hovering over the waters. And God said, "Let there be light," and there was light. God saw that the light was good, and he separated the light from the darkness. God called the light "day," and the darkness he called "night." And there was evening, and there was morning—the first day."*

—Gen. 1:1-5.

The Bible begins with "In the Beginning…" It emphasizes the beginning of all things—matter, time and space. Rather than being a summary statement, this is part of the actual narrative of creation. The creation of matter began at the beginning of all things. Elohim (the plural name for God) created the heavens—deep space, dark matter, the backdrop for the stars, planets, the moon and sun.

Then God created the Earth. The creation of the heavens and Earth are not an overview of the first day of creation but two separate acts of creation—first space, then the Earth. The earth began without form, and it was empty of land, animals or any objects other than a watery mixture from which God would separate into dry ground. The earth would have been formed with a core of magma that was surrounded by the watery mixture. The water would have cooled the magma and formed the crust under the water.

The heavens and the Earth were in complete darkness. Then God said there should be light. What exactly did God create at this moment? God said he created the sun, moon and stars on day four, so what was the light source? We know it was not the light of God Himself. His light is everywhere, so that light cannot be hidden or blocked off.

The best explanation is that God created light: $C = f\lambda$, and there was ($c = f\lambda$,) light

C: represents the speed of light (approximately 3.00×10^8 m/s)

f: represents the frequency of the light wave.

λ: (lambda) represents the wavelength of the light wave.

Light is a form of electromagnetic radiation that is visible to the human eye. It travels as waves and can also be described as tiny packets of energy called photons. The speed of light is a constant, approximately 186,000 miles per second in a vacuum. The colors we perceive are determined by the wavelength of the light.

In what form did the light appear? It could have been a globe, like the sun. What we know for sure is that it came from a single source and did not entirely fill deep space. In its nature this light would not have differed from our sun or any star in the galaxy. It would have sustained plant life and functioned as our sun does today.

Next, God separated light from darkness. This was not a physical separation but a designation. He identified the light as daytime and the darkness as night.

The light shone from one direction and struck the face of the earth facing the light. The other side of the earth was in darkness. This declaration is further clarified when He defines a day as half-light and half-darkness (evening and morning), the first day of all the days that follow for all time. So, the Universe began in darkness and came into the light. Evening and morning equaled a 24-hour day.

When God created the sun, moon and stars on day four, He either used the light he created on day one, placing it in each star, or He created the light each time he made a new star.[85]

Verse 2 indicates the earth was rotating and that everything was in darkness. In verses 9-13, God gathers the waters into one place and dry ground appears. He then causes the land to produce vegetation and seed-bearing plants and fruit of all kinds.

In verses 14-19, the sun and stars are created. God had already created a light source. He places its light within the celestial bodies he had created on day four.

On day five, God creates water creatures and birds. Great creatures of the sea, the earth and the sky are filled with such beings, and again this is described as evening and morning.

Finally, God creates land creatures of all kinds. The creation of all animals on sea and land would have included the dinosaurs. He finishes by creating Adam and Eve. He provides their diet, every seed-bearing tree and all seed-eating plants. He calls His creation "very good" and reminds us again of His definition of a day as evening and morning.

The Meaning of Day

"These are the generations of the heavens and the earth when they were created, in the day that the Lord God made the earth and the heavens."

—Genesis 2:4.

"In the day" refers to the creation referenced is verse 1 when God created the heavens then the earth. The subsequent days

---

85   www.youtube.com/results?search_query=dr+petrovich

   Bridging the Origins Divide

focused on filling the Earth and the creation of living entities.

The latest theory is that Genesis is less about the creation of matter than bringing order out of chaos.[86] This view is espoused by Danial Kim of Talbot Seminary and John Walton of Wheaton College. Recently, "The Holy Post Podcast" promoted this view in an episode entitled, "Does the Bible Say That the Earth is 6,000 years old?"[87]

In their presentation, the Holy Post sets up a strawman argument saying that "to understand the bible we must understand the language, style of communication, figures of speech and cultural understandings" of the author and audience. They say the Bible was not written *to* us but *for* us. Their primary point is that we need to know what the ancient Israelites believed concerning creation so we can understand what Moses was saying.

They present these ideas as if they are special and unique to only their points of view. However, these ideas are basic principles of Bible interpretation which all Bible students follow. There are several problems with their approach. While culture and language can assist in interpreting the text, in the end they completely ignore the text and use what they believe the culture around Israel believed as the primary basis for their interpretation.

These professors believe that these ancient cultures saw creation as a process of bringing order out of chaos rather than the creation of matter and that the ancient Israelites thought more like ancient Egyptians, Babylonians and Sumerians than modern Americans.

They also claim that Young Earth Creationism is primarily an American school of thought. However, it began with Euro-

------

86   "www.youtube.com/watch?v=4A4ab-ldKqE
87   IBID

peans and early scientists such as Newton, Kepler, Bacon, Pacal, Petty and Boyle to name a few. For about the past 400 years, almost everyone believed in a young earth.

Jewish thought and theology were unlike any in the world, including the beliefs of the Ancient Near East (ANE) communities. The "order from chaos" theory reflects a naturalistic view of the Scriptures which sees Israel as progressing from polytheism to theism in the same manner as other nations. This is simply not true, nor is it a reflection of who the people of God were. From the beginning, God chose individuals from Seth's bloodline, a righteous lineage to whom God had been communicating His truth and perspective from their beginning.

Moses was not writing to Jews who were steeped in the cultures around them. He was telling us God's account of His creation. He was not just writing God's words to Israel, but to the people in cultures around them. God did not begin with the Jews; he began with the righteous line of Seth and the other patriarchs. The information he gave them was passed on from generation to generation. Israel did not exist when God created the heavens and the Earth. Moses was not making up his own story to counter the cultures around him. He was communicating to all humanity God's story, His worldview, His plans, His intentions for us all. The word of God is not reactionary; it is corrective and clarifying not just for Israel but all cultures for all time.

The podcasters say the Genesis record of creation does not focus on the creation of matter—rocks, trees, deserts, etc.—but on bringing order out of creation. They say that Genesis 1 does not start with nothing but with God hovering over the waters. This contradicts "In the beginning God created the heavens

 Bridging the Origins Divide

and the earth." Are not the heavens and the earth primarily composed of matter, rocks, trees and water?

Each day, God shaped and formed another part of the material world. Danial and John claim that Christian scientist Isaac Newton and James Ussher, who famously dated creation's chronology of the universe, forced their scientific worldview on the text, saying the ancient Jews would never have asked the questions modern man asks. They state, "When did God create all the stuff? God never inspires the writer to answer this because it is not a question the ancient Israelites would want to be answered."

I label this wishful exegesis and scriptural nullification. By making bold statements about what secular cultures in the ANE believed and declaring the Genesis record is on the same plane as these other cultures, they basically eradicated the Genesis record. Why? Ultimately, because it gives them another way to interpret Genesis that does not contradict the beliefs of science. Finally, it ignores all the other passages about creation, specifically John 1:3 where John says of Jesus that everything which came into being came into being by the word "Jesus."

Chapter Nine

Why a Young Earth Matters

A common response when discussing the age of the earth is that it does not make any difference. "If God is the Creator, then who cares?" This is usually accompanied by statements which either denounce the Bible as an unscientific textbook, or their view of Genesis 1 removes the conflict between an old and young earth. Every few years we hear new interpretations of Genesis that attempt to remove or nullify the apparent conflict between science and creationism.

> *"The sooner the Christian community gets rid of young earth creationism the better. This is an embarrassment for the Christian Faith and is creating enormous obstacles to Christian belief among scientifically educated people. The earth and universe are not 6,000 years old and there's no reason biblically to think there is! We really need to shed ourselves of this as a Christian community."*[88]

—William Lane Craig

If the Bible is the word of God, then it must be the foundation for our understanding of the creation of the heavens and the earth. If the earth is truly billions of years old and the scientific perspective of creation can be proven, then the Bible and our understanding of Genesis is wrong, and the Bible would not be the inspired word of God.

If the earth is billions of years old, millions of animals and other living creatures must have died before sin entered the world. The consequence of Adam and Eve's sin was death. The was the essence of the Adamic Covenant, God's agreement with Adam and Eve.

Did God really say, "You must not eat from any tree in the garden?"

"The woman said to the serpent, 'We may eat fruit from the trees in the garden, but God did say, "You must not eat fruit from the tree that is in the middle of the garden, and you must not touch it, or you will die."'

'You will not certainly die,' the serpent said to the woman. 'For God knows that when you eat from it your eyes will be opened, and you will be like God, knowing good and evil.'"

—Genesis 3:1-f

"Therefore, just as sin came into the world through one man, and death through sin, and so death spread to all men because all have sinned— for sin indeed was in the world before the law was given, but sin is not counted where there is no law. 14 Yet death reigned from Adam to Moses, even over those whose sinning was not like the

*transgression of Adam, who was a type of the one who was
to come."*

—Rom.12:12-14

The Apostle Paul tells us that death came to the world because
of the sin and rebellion of Adam and Eve. The centerpiece of the
gospel message is the redemption of humanity from our sins
and the effects of our sin on the world.

> *"For the creation waits with eager longing for the reveal-
> ing of the sons of God. For the creation was subjected to
> futility, not willingly, but because of him who subjected
> it, in hope that the creation itself will be set free from
> its bondage to corruption and obtain the freedom of the
> glory of the children of God. For we know that the whole
> creation has been groaning together in the pains of child-
> birth until now."*

—Romans 8:20-22

If the Scriptures are to be taken seriously, there can be no death
before the Fall. However, any view of an old earth requires the
death of billions of animals and living things from the beginning
of time. According to the Scriptures, the first death recorded
was the sacrificial death of an animal whose skin God used to
clothe Adam and Eve's nakedness after their sin.

> *"And the Lord God made for Adam and for his wife gar-
> ments of skins and clothed them."*

—Genesis 3:21.

This death was to cover their sin from the Fall.

What about the death of other life forms before the Fall, not
just dinosaurs but all the bacteria and other unseen deaths? The
fact is there would have been no death of any form of life.

                                    Bridging the Origins Divide

Also, it is likely the Fall took place quite quickly after the completion of the creation week. If it did not happen quickly, it would mean that Adam & Eve either did not have sexual relations until after the Fall, or God kept them from pregnancy until after the Fall. Otherwise, their children would have been sinless, and the whole process would have needed to be done again.

The Scriptures teach a young earth.

The clearest and best exegetical understanding of Genesis is that God created everything in six solar days. Of course, this creates a serious conflict with the conventional model of the big bang and billions of years of time for the creation of the heavens and earth. Many theologians have tried to resolve this conflict by interpreting "day" as something other than a 24-hour solar day or by adding long ages of time between verses 1 & 2. Some claim it is just poetry and not a literal creation. However, Genesis 1 and 2 are not the only passages that describe a six-day creation. Statements from Jesus support a young earth and six-day creation.

> *"Jesus replied. 'But at the beginning of creation God made them male and female. For this reason, a man will leave his father and mother and be united to his wife, and the two will become one flesh. So, they are no longer two, but one flesh. Therefore, what God has joined together, let no one separate.'"*

> —Mark 10:6-9

Jesus makes a similar statement in Matthew:

> *Some Pharisees came to him to test him. They asked, "Is it lawful for a man to divorce his wife for any and every reason?"*

> *"Haven't you read," he replied, "that at the beginning the*

Creator made them male and female and said, 'For this reason a man will leave his father and mother and be united to his wife, and the two will become one flesh. So, they are no longer two, but one flesh. Therefore, what God has joined together, let no one separate.'?"

—Matthew 19:3-6

Jesus quotes from Genesis 1:27:

"So, God created mankind in his own image, in the image of God he created them; male and female he created them."

Then he adds the phrase, *"at the beginning of Creation,"* signifying the first days of creation. Both statements undermine any theory that adds millions of years to the creation account. Again, there cannot be 4.5 billion years between the creation of the earth and the creation of Adam and Eve.

Moses defines what he meant by a "day" in Exodus:

Remember the Sabbath day, to keep it holy. Six days you shall labor, and do all your work, but the seventh day is a Sabbath to the Lord your God. On it you shall not do any work, you, or your son, or your daughter, your male servant, or your female servant, or your livestock, or the sojourner who is within your gates. For in six days the Lord made heaven and earth, the sea, and all that is in them, and rested on the seventh day. Therefore, the Lord blessed the Sabbath day and made it holy.

—Exodus 20:8-11

And the Lord said to Moses, "You are to speak to the people of Israel and say, 'Above all you shall keep my Sabbaths, for this is a sign between me and you throughout

Bridging the Origins Divide

The sabbath referred to in these passages is a 24-hour day. Moses makes very clear what he meant by "day" in Genesis 1 and 2.

Adding long ages of time does not solve the conflict with science. If we can add long ages of time to the Genesis record, we can reconcile creationism with the latest scientific theory. The problem is that the entire Genesis account is filled with supernatural creative activity.

Imposing billions of years into the biblical text may seem to mitigate the conflict, but it does not fit the scientific narrative. To avoid a conflict with an eventual human theory of evolution, God could have simply said, "In the beginning God created the heavens and the earth." Period. We reinterpret the Bible every time science believes they have solved the mystery of creation. In essence, we are always playing defense, trying to defend the Bible from the latest "scientific proof."

From the perspective of an evolutionary world view, Day

1 was 13.9 billion of our days. Earth came into existence 4.5 billion years before the creation of the heavens and earth. All this and subsequent creations had to be caused. Science cannot explain how these things happened, but by their faith in the big bang and other theories, they believe they have.

You cannot harmonize Genesis with the scientific world-view simply by adding millions of years of time to chapters 1 and 2. Adding time is a weak attempt to reconcile science and the Bible. The interpretation of the text is overwhelming, and it distorts the narrative of Genesis 1-11. Changing the meaning of one word does not reconcile the narrative.

Science claims the earth was once molten lava that cooled over billions of years.

> *"The earth was formed out of water and by water, by the same waters the world of that day was deluged and destroyed."*
>
> *—2 Peter 3:6.*

Additionally, the order of creation is different. God created space, deep space, then the earth on day one. He also created light before the sun moon and stars, and He created birds before mammals, to name a few differences.

Peter's prophecies tell us in the last days that the deception of evolution will be accepted on the earth. He foretold the lie of an old Earth and that an evolutionary worldview would have great sway in the last days.

> *Above all, you must understand that in the last days scoffers will come, scoffing and following their own evil desires. They will say, "Where is this coming he promised? Ever since our ancestors died, everything goes on as it has since the beginning of creation." But they delib-*

erately forget that long ago by God's word the heavens
came into being and the earth was formed out of water
and by water. By these waters also the world of that time
was deluged and destroyed. By the same word the present
heavens and earth are reserved for fire, being kept for the
day of judgment and destruction of the ungodly.

—2 Peter 3:3-7

The Church no longer speaks with authority.

There was a time when 12 men turned the world on its head, and Jesus's word was law. The spiritual influence of the church has been in flux over the centuries. Initially, the church wielded great spiritual influence, then it changed to political power and became part of the governmental system.

We came to rely on this political power and the government to accomplish spiritual things. Then the Church became a part of the state and eventually became the state. One could say the Church was God with its word ruling everything. The church eventually lost its influence, and its power converted to science. The Church had been God; now science had become God, and the Church capitulated.

We now speak without authority. Our power is in the proclamation of the gospel, the teaching of His word and the power of the Holy Spirit.

God spoke and created the entire universe out of nothing. The word of God is powerful and sharper than any two-edged sword. The Scriptures are God's very words to humanity; only His word will change our world.

Science declares that Earth is billions of years old. I declare that the heavens and earth are not billions of years old and call upon the body of Christ to believe in the Scriptures. Scientific beliefs are based entirely on the opinions of men who have rejected a supernatural worldview and the evidence of Scripture. They have denied a global flood and its implications and have fallen into error.

Millions have lost their faith.

Many older believers have resolved their conflicts between the Bible and evolution. However, millions still struggle with the questions they have not resolved and may never find their way to faith.

Evolution and higher criticism destroyed the faith in Europe. You may have found your faith despite evolution theory and its long ages, but millions have lost their faith, especially young people. Deconstruction is one of the latest movements in the Church. Huge numbers of young and old are deconstructing their faith, re-examining and walking away from Jesus in large part because of the lies of evolution and the conflict with Genesis.

In his book, *Already Gone,* Ken Hamm discusses the reasons so many young people are leaving the faith. For one, the story of Noah's ark and a global flood do not seem to align with the long ages of evolution theory. It is considered scholarly to reject faith in favor of reason. Religion is blind ignorance, while science is intelligent reason.[89]

It undermines Genesis 1-11.

The early history of humanity is recorded in the first 11 chapters of Genesis. It covers the creation of the world, humanity, sin and fall of man, marriage, God's judgment through a global flood, and division of the nations. The Bible teaches that God

---

89 answersingenesis.org/church/pew-research-why-young-people-leaving-christianity/

     Bridging the Origins Divide

destroyed the world with a global flood. Most scientists reject this along with many old Earth Christians. The Bible teaches that humans lived over 900 years of age before the Flood. This too is rejected by science in the same manner as a six-day creation. The Bible teaches that God fragmented our languages at Babel and separated humanity into different groups, nations and ethnicities. This is also rejected by science.

If we accept that God made the heavens and the earth in six days out of nothing, it changes the contemporary narrative about God. Since the advent of evolution and an old earth, God as creator has taken a backseat; he has become a side note in the discussion about creation. It also underscores the arrogance and foolishness of scientists and philosophers whose paradigm must otherwise remain sacrosanct.

Has science proven the earth is billions of years old or that all life spawned from a single-celled organism? Which is true—the biblical record or the conjecture of science? The burden of proof rests on science; can they prove their claims? The theory of an old Earth and Heaven is based on the suppositions of the scientific community.

Chapter Ten

The Greatest Lie Ever Told

Hutton, Lyell, & Darwin—At History's Crossroads

James Hutton, Charles Lyell, Charles Darwin and Julius Wellhausen came together at a crossroads in history. It was a time when the so-called great thinkers were questioning religion, government, social constructs and all power regimes. Humanity would either return to and follow the Scriptures or set a new course away from a biblical worldview into a fully secular society. They did not abandon the biblical perspective immediately, but in less than century a naturalistic, anti-supernatural philosophy began to rule most of the scientific and educational communities. Their beliefs and deceptions radically changed the foundational philosophies of the world. Their teachings undermined the philosophical underpinnings of the Christian faith.

James Hutton, often called the father of geology, concocted the greatest lie ever told. He proclaimed (without concrete evidence) that the heavens and earth were infinitely old and that a six-day creation was not true. His proclamation was based on his observation and belief that the earth looked much older than the Bible indicated.

He rejected the idea that the geology of the earth was formed through catastrophic events such as a global flood. Instead, he developed the theory of uniformitarianism, even though there was no scientific evidence for it. He assumed the earth's rate of erosion and lift had always been the same, just as scientists today believe the .08 inches yearly of continental drift has always been the same.

> *"The past history of our globe must be explained by what can be seen to be happening now. No powers are to be employed that are not natural to the globe, no action to be admitted except those of which we know the principle."*[90]

Today's speculation on age is now 13.5 billion years for the universe and 4.5 billion for the earth. These numbers are based primarily on the assumptions of naturalism, uniformity and deeply flawed modern dating techniques.[91]

In 1778, concerning the creation of the earth, Hutton famously stated that there is no vestige of a beginning and no prospect of an end.[92] Essentially, this would indicate the earth is eternal, which is a belief held by Aristotle and others.

Hutton was a deist. He believed in a god who created the world then left it to operate by its own natural laws. He believed

---

90 "Transactions of the Royal Society of Edinburgh

91 Up to the discovery of radiometric dating, everything they believed was unproven, how excited they must have to finally have some evidence for their wild speculation about the age of the earth.

92 "Theory of the earth; or an investigation of the laws observable in the composition, dissolution and restoration of land upon the globe. (From. the Trans., Roy. soc. of Edinb.).", p.96

in a God that does not intervene in human affairs. He believed that the present earth was formed from an earlier earth that was destroyed by the natural process of erosion over long periods of time.

Hutton's theory of uniformitarianism states that all natural processes we see today have always been the same. Erosion took place slowly, and layers of rock are slowly re-laid over millions of years.

> *"Hutton described a universe very different from the Biblical cosmos: one formed by a continuous cycle in which rocks and soil are washed into the sea, compacted into bedrock, forced up to the surface by volcanic processes, and eventually worn away into sediment once again. "The result, therefore, of this physical enquiry," Hutton concluded, "is that we find no vestige of a beginning, no prospect of an end."[93]*

> *Hutton believed in the Theory of Uniformitarianism [...] the belief that geological forces at work in the present day [...] are the same as those that operated in the past [...] Hutton's theories amounted to a frontal attack on a popular contemporary school of thought called catastrophism: the belief that only catastrophes, such as the Great Flood, could account for the form and nature of a 6,000-year-old Earth."[94]*

Charles Lyell was intent on undermining the Genesis record and the role it played in geology. He eventually became Hutton's primary spokesman. Terry Mortenson states the following

---

93 simple.wikipedia.org/wiki/James_Hutton

94 www.amnh.org/learn-teach/curriculum-collections/earth-inside-and-out/james-hutton

Bridging the Origins Divide

in his book, *The Great Turning Point: The Church's Catastrophic Mistake on Geology—Before Darwin:*

"In his private correspondence, Lyell wrote in a letter to fellow old-earth geologist Roderick Murchison: I trust I shall make my sketch of the progress of geology popular. Old [Rev. John Fleming] is frightened and thinks the age will not stand my anti-Mosaical conclusions and at least that the subject will for a time become unpopular and awkward for the clergy, but I am not afraid. I shall out with the whole but in as conciliatory a manner as possible. ...If we don't irritate, which I fear that we may (though mere history), we shall carry all with us. If you don't triumph over them but compliment the liberality and candor of the present age, the bishops and enlightened saints will join us in despising both the ancient and modern physio-theologians. It is just the time to strike, so rejoice that, sinner as you are, the Q.R. is open to you.[95]

"P.S. ... I conceived the idea five or six years ago [1824–25], that if ever the Mosaic geology could be set down without giving offence, it would be in an historical sketch, and you must abstract mine, in order to have as little to say as possible yourself. Let them feel it and point the moral.[96]

"Lyell, the lawyer par excellence, was involved, not in scientific investigation but political game playing to ensure his uniformitarian ideas would be accepted by the

---

95 IBID
96 creation.com/the-hidden-agenda-of-charles-lyell-was-to-free-science-from-moses from Mortenson, T., The Great Turning Point: The Church's Catastrophic Mistake on Geology—Before Darwin, Master Books, Inc., P.O. Box 726, Green Forest, AR 72638, USA, 2004, pp. 226–227, citing Lyell, Katherine (Lyell's sister-in-law), Life, Letters and Journals of Sir Charles Lyell, Bart. (London: Murray, 1881), I:p. 268–271.

church, even though he knew they clearly contradicted the plain teaching of Scripture." The physical part of geological inquiry ought to be conducted as if the Scriptures were not in existence.[97]

"Lyell's secretive scheming not only deceived the church to accept his false ideas that undermined the Gospel, but he set geology on a wrong path for over a century, as geologists now recognize: "Lyell also sold geology some snake oil. He convinced geologists that ... all past processes acted at essentially their current rates (that is, those observed in historical time). This extreme gradualism has led to numerous unfortunate consequences, including the rejection of sudden or catastrophic events in the face of positive evidence for them, for no reason other than that they were not gradual."[98]

These beliefs set the stage for the lie that has gripped the scientific community for two centuries. Their intentional deception became the foundation used to make decisions on the age of the earth from that point forward. Charles Darwin has said he owes everything to Charles Lyell. At his death in 1875, he said:

"I never forget that almost everything which I have done in science I owe to the study of his great works, and the science of geology is enormously indebted to Lyell—more so, as I believe, than to any other man who ever lived.[99]

Charles Darwin answered a straightforward question concerning his belief in God and the Bible. The question centered on

---

97 Lyell further promulgated his uniformitarian views in a lecture at King's College, London, on 4 May 1832
98 Allmon, W.D. Post Gradualism, Science 262:122–123, October 1, 1993
99 Charles Darwin Francis Darwin, ed., The Life and Letters of Charles Darwin, (1887)

                    Bridging the Origins Divide

whether reading his books would affect his faith in Christianity.

> *"Dear Sir, I am sorry to have to inform you that I do not believe in the Bible as a divine revelation & therefore not in Jesus Christ as the son of God."*[100]

Clearly, Darwin's faith was directly undermined by his own philosophy. He was but the first of millions who lost their faith by accepting the deception of evolution and long ages of time. While none of these men claimed to be atheists, they were in fact practical atheists. Their world view was centered on the idea that God had nothing to with the creation of the heavens and earth. Everything they proposed was based on a natural, anti-supernatural belief system which must explain all things without invoking a divine being. They were responsible for the separation of science from faith.

Evolution and old earth theories were around long before Lyell and Darwin popularized their hypotheses. Darwin's father wrote a book which Charles used in developing his theory of evolution. The development of long ages of time by Lyell and Hutton were not new, but this was a pathway to control the scientific and religious communities.

For almost two centuries, long ages of geological time have been pushed and drilled into the minds of an unsuspecting world. Over this time, the historic Christian worldview has been radically impacted by this "scientific" dogma. These beliefs directly contradict the clearest understanding of Genesis 1 and 2 along with numerous supportive passages in the Bible—Exodus 20:11, 31:17, Matthew 19:3-6, Mark 10:6-9. These scientific claims are false and are an assault on the inspiration and authority of the Scriptures.

---

100 IBID

The Documentary Hypothesis questions Moses's authorship of the Torah (first five books of the Old Testament). Higher Criticism questions the authorship, dates and literary structure of whole Bible. However, it was Julius Wellhausen who popularized the anti-Mosaic authorship of the Torah. Wellhausen presented the faith as a superstitious religion with made-up stories; he had a clear anti-supernatural belief system. James Hutton opened the door for Lyell who opened the door for Darwin who opened the door for Wellhausen.

Together these men successfully undermined the Genesis record of Creation along with the inspiration and authority of the Scriptures. This led many European and American Christians to lose their faith, and it has had a disastrous effect on popular culture since.

Perhaps it is understandable for atheists and anti-Christian secular scientists to proclaim these ideas as hard facts. Unfortunately, they are not alone. The mantra of an old earth has been accepted and proclaimed by Christian men and women in the fields of science just as vehemently. They often mock Young Earth believers more than secular scientists.

Christian apologist Dr. William Lane Craig (a man I like and whose materials I have used in apologetic discussions) said,

"The sooner the Christian community gets rid of young earth creationism the better. This is an embarrassment for the Christian Faith and is creating enormous obstacles to Christian belief among scientifically educated people. The earth and universe are not 6,000 years old and there's no reason biblically to think there is! We really need to shed ourselves of this as a Christian community." [101]

---

101 www.youtube.com/watch?v=p5XGWMOrLQU

     Bridging the Origins Divide

There has been a gradual decay in the Christian faith for the past five centuries. The Body of Christ is clearly divided and weakened by the doctrine of an old earth. In universities and progressive churches, millions have walked away from the faith. Even strong otherwise evangelical believers are compromised by the long ages of deep time.

As it was in the beginning of science, there remain strong, biblically based scientists who reject the lies of an old earth, though they are mocked and ridiculed by Old Earth believers. Princeton, Harvard, Oxford and other once strong and vibrant Christian universities are now a hotbed of anti-Christian world views.

Two significant events took place involving Galileo and Copernicus and Charles Lyell and Charles Darwin.

Copernicus, Galileo and Sir Francis Bacon

The controversy over geocentrism (the sun revolves around Earth) versus heliocentrism (Earth revolves around the sun) and between Galileo, Copernicus and the Catholic church set the stage for the present-day conflict between faith and science. These were 15th century theories regarding the movement of Earth and the sun.

Geocentrism was taught by Aristotle and almost universally accepted by everyone. In 1543, Copernicus published *On the Revolutions of the Heavenly Spheres*. He concluded that Earth was not the center of the universe as the church believed; rather the sun was. When Galileo supported this theory in part, he was charged with heresy and placed on house arrest.

The response by the Church became a great embarrassment to scientists. It was trying to defend the centrality of humanity as the centerpiece of God's plan and thus saw Earth's location as a symbol of this belief. All involved parties believed Jesus came to earth to save humanity.

Heliocentrism represented a momentous change for the religious and scientific communities. The Catholic church did not handle the situation well, but it was reasonable to question the new theory. A cursory reading of Psalms 19 appears to indicate that the sun revolves around Earth.

"In the heavens God has pitched a tent for the sun. It is like a bridegroom coming out of his chamber, like a champion rejoicing to run his course. It rises at one end of the heavens and makes its circuit to the other; nothing is deprived of its warmth."

—Psalm 19:4-6.

"He set the earth on its foundations so that it should never be moved."

—Psalms 104:5

Galileo's punishment had a profound effect on him and many others. The primary impact of this conflict was the fear of challenging new beliefs presented by science. As a result, he built a subtle but significant philosophical wall between religion and science, saying,

"The intention of the Holy Ghost is to teach us how to go to heaven, not how heaven goes." [102]

In other words, the Bible teaches theology and morality but not astronomy or science. Along with Galileo, Sir Francis Bacon held to a young earth and six-day creation, but after this event he was reluctant to challenge science on the details. Sir Francis Bacon said,

"Some of the moderns, however, have indulged in this

---

102 Galileo, Letter to the Grand Duchess Christina (1615

                    Bridging the Origins Divide

folly, with such consummate carelessness, as to have endeavored to find a natural philosophy on the first chapter of Genesis, the book of Job, and other passages of holy Scripture— 'seeking the dead among the living.' And this folly is the more to be prevented and restrained, because, from the unsound admixture of things divine and human, there arises not merely a fantastic philosophy, but also a heretical religion. [103]

The Bible does not teach geocentrism. Psalm 19 is poetry and is written from the perspective of one who lives on Earth and has never been in space. They are figurative statements that reflect the centrality of humanity in God's economy. Regardless, the resulting debacle unnecessarily drove a wedge between church leaders and the scientific community.

These and similar reactions have led many Christians to hesitate to disagree with the opinions of science. From the first presentation by Hutton and Lyell, there were Christian scientists who felt the need to harmonize the two contradictory accounts of creation. It was Christian scientists who developed the supposed ages of the geological column. While we should attempt to understand fully the biblical record and harmonize it with science, it is not always possible.

For the Bible to be the Word of God, there can be no contradictions between absolute facts of science and factual statements of the Bible. This means that if science can absolutely prove the Bible is in error regarding statements of substance, then biblical authority can legitimately be questioned.

However, there are questions that may never be answered

---

103 Francis Bacon, translated by Andrew Johnson from the 1620 original Novum Organum, London, p. 43, 1859

about past processes based on scientific speculation. We are not obligated to answer every question and satisfy every critic of the biblical record. An unanswered question does not mean the Bible is wrong, only that some things cannot be known with absolute certainty.

We are not obligated to prove how the Creator made the universe. It has no relevance unless science can conclusively demonstrate the process used and how it directly conflicts with biblical revelation.

We must be wary of compromising biblical teaching in favor of ever-changing claims of science. Unfortunately, many are quick to abandon its teachings and turn to science as the final word in such conflicts.

Natural Revelation vs. Special Revelation

Christian doctrine teaches that God has spoken to humanity through two sources: natural revelation and special revelation. Natural revelation is observable data in nature.

> *"The heavens declare the glory of God; the skies proclaim the work of his hands. Day after day they pour forth speech; night after night they reveal knowledge."*
>
> —Psalms 19:1-2

> *"Since what may be known about God is plain to them, because God has made it plain to them. For since the creation of the world God's invisible qualities—his eternal power and divine nature—have been clearly seen, being understood from what has been made, so that people are without excuse."*
>
> —Romans 1:19-20

Special revelation is the belief that the Scriptures are God's

Bridging the Origins Divide

direct communication to humanity. They give us specific information concerning the primary doctrines of the faith such as the mission and message of Jesus and His crucifixion and resurrection, the deity of Christ, the Holy Spirit and the nature of God, the history of the nation of Israel, and the creation of the world and all living things. These are doctrines known only by special revelation.

> *"For the word of God is alive and active. Sharper than any double-edged sword, it penetrates even dividing soul and spirit, joints and marrow; it judges the thoughts and attitudes of the heart. Nothing in all creation is hidden from God's sight. Everything is uncovered and laid bare before the eyes of him to whom we must give account."*
>
> —Hebrews 4:12-13

God's Two Books

Thomas Brown (1605–1682) wrote,

> *"There are two books from whence I collect my divinity: besides that, one written of God, another of his servant, nature, that universal and public manuscript that lies expansed (seen) unto the eyes of all"*[104]

Almost 500 years later, scholars and laypeople alike write about and personally remind me of the Galileo debacle and that believing in a young earth is just as foolish as believing in geocentrism.

Galileo, Bacon and many others believed there were two books from God: science and the Bible. Are there two books of God?

---

104 www.encyclopedia.com

It seems better to say there are two means of communication from the Creator—the Bible and nature. To put science on the same level as the Bible is dangerous, but it is exactly what has taken place since the days of Galileo.

The deception of the two-book belief system is in comparing science with the Bible, especially speculative theories concerning the origin of the earth. Natural revelation cannot definitively tell us the age of the earth. When science discovers a demonstrable truth, it should be considered part of God's revelation. Scientific opinions are not facts and fall short of divine revelation.

Galileo grew skeptical about the bible and Science.

"Galileo viewed scientific descriptions in the Bible as not important, for the common man could not understand them."[105]

Peter's Prophecy

Charles Lyell predicted he could convince biblical scholars to buy into the lie of a uniformitarian old earth geology, and he was right. However, the Apostle Peter prophesied almost 2,000 years ago that Charles Lyell and men like him would one day teach the very lies that they spread.

"Above all, you must understand that in the last days scoffers will come, scoffing and following their own evil desires. They will say, "Where is this 'coming' he promised? Ever since our ancestors died, everything goes on as it has since the beginning of creation." But they deliberately forget that long ago by God's word the heavens came into being and the earth was formed out of water

---

105 IBID

      Bridging the Origins Divide

*and by water. By these waters also the world of that time
was deluged and destroyed. By the same word the present
heavens and earth are reserved for fire, being kept for the
day of judgment and destruction of the ungodly."*

—2 Peter 3:3-7

Peter's prophecy covered four ideas:

Uniformity — James Hutton's theory. *"Everything goes on as it
has since the beginning of creation."* Geological processes have
always been the same. Radiometric decay has always been at
the same rate. Erosion and uplift have always been the same.

Uniformity is a significant point of departure from ortho-
doxy and is the basis for evolution and the long ages of time
it proposes. Every estimate of age is based on the belief that
natural processes we observe today have always been the same.
Radioactive decay, the speed of light, continental drift and the
rate of accumulation in Iceland's snowpack are all based on the
assumption of slow gradual geological change.

The rejection of catastrophism and the Genesis flood are
key events in the history of evolution. Initially, all catastrophic
events were rejected along with the flood. Over time, evidence
for catastrophic events was so overwhelming that scientists
were forced to include some catastrophes along with their
understanding of the earth's geology.

However, they have never revisited the theory of a worldwide flood as the cause of the earth's geology. Instead, their latest guess is that a great meteor destroyed the earth and killed
off the dinosaurs. The problem is that natural selection and big
bang theories are all based on assumptions of *uniformity and
naturalism.*

Anti-Supernaturalism — *"They deliberately forget that long ago by God's Word the heavens came into being and were formed out of water and by water."* Science by its very definition can only test things that already exist; they can only speculate about what might have happened in the past. The creation of the world was a supernatural event: God spoke the heavens into being. When God spoke everything into existence, he also established the laws that govern his creations. These laws can be studied, but we must consider the supernatural aspect of their existence.

Naturalism — *"The heavens came into being, and the earth was formed out of water and by water."* This is the belief that we can only discover the process of creation through the examination of what we see today. The rejection of the supernatural means you must speculate about what happened in the past—the big bang theory, multi-verses, etc. Many scientists consider these theories as fact not because they have been proven so, but because in their minds they are the only explanations that can be considered without acknowledging a Creator. Anti- supernatural bias limits the ability to see what is apparent.

Anti-Catastrophism — *"By these waters also the world of that time was deluged and destroyed."* …resulting in the rejection of a global flood and initially all possible geological catastrophes. The rejection of the Flood and other catastrophes enabled science to come up with outlandish theories about the geology of the earth.

Because of these suppositions, they also reject the impending destruction of the earth. *"By the same word the present heavens and earth are reserved for fire, being kept for the day of judgment and destruction of the ungodly."*

 Bridging the Origins Divide

Radiometric and Other Dating Techniques

The greatest challenge to the biblical record of creation is the purported age of the heavens and the earth. Since Georges Comte De Buffon's 1788 AD proposal of an age of 75,000 years,[106] we have seen age estimates grow exponentially. Since the end of the 19th century, it has grown from 100 million years to 20 billion.

The latest radical theory is that the universe is at least 986 billion years older than physicists thought. The revolutionary study suggests that time did not begin with the big bang 14 billion years ago. This mammoth explosion which created all the matter we see around us was only one of many.[107]

These "scientific" calculations are continually in flux. They are only estimates based on the latest observation of the stars or the rocks. For instance, the age of the universe is based on calculations that it would take light from the farthest known point in the universe 13 to 20 billion years to reach Earth. Since we can see this light, the deduction is that the universe is at least that many years old.[108]

However, the age of the earth is completely speculative and is based on the belief that it and our solar system were simultaneously formed from condensed interstellar stardust. The earth was once a molten fireball, so its primordial rocks cannot be dated. Instead, scientists use meteorites.

Meteorites are thought to be remnants of a planet which broke up prior to our solar system's formation. The pieces of meteorites that have fallen to earth are supposedly 4.6 billion years old. Hence, the age of the earth is approximately the same.[109] Scientists claim the geological column, along with

---

106 Georges Comte de Buffon, Les epoques de la nature, Paris, 1778.
107 www.guardian.co.uk/science/2006/may/05/spaceexploration.universe
108 I have not attempted to answer the speed of light question
109 geology.wr.usgs.gov/parks/gtime/ageofearth.

radiometric potassium argon and other dating methods, prove that the earth is hundreds of millions of years old.

The development of long geological ages and the theory of evolution were a direct result of the rejection of the biblical record of creation. Since the Bible gives us the approximate age of the universe and that God was the source of everything, what is gained by an attempt to determine the age and method of creation? Certainly, Lyell intended to undermine the authority and reliability of the Bible.

Atheists and other scientists also rejected the claims of Lyell and Hutton. Men like Stephen Jay Gould and Derek Agar did not hold to the strict long ages of geologic time.

> *"Gradualism was never proved from the rocks by Lyell and Darwin but was rather imposed with bias upon nature. It has had a profoundly negative impact by stifling hypotheses and by closing the minds of a profession toward reasonable empirical alternatives to the dogma of gradualism. Lyell won with rhetoric what he could not carry with data."*
>
> —Stephen Jay Gould.[110]

Derek Agar, famed atheist, said,

> *"Just as politicians rewrite human history, so geologists rewrite earth history. For a century and a half, the geological world has been dominated, one might even say brainwashed, by the gradualistic uniformitarianism of Charles Lyell. Any suggestion of catastrophic events has been rejected as old-fashioned, unscientific and even laughable."[111]*

---

110 Catastrophes and Earth History (1984)
111 Derek Ager, The New Catastrophism (1993)

Has science proven the heavens and earth are billions of years old?

We should only reject the biblical record if science can prove conclusively that the Bible is wrong. Has science proved the earth is billions of years old? Most scientists believe they have absolute proof for its long ages. You cannot read *National Geographic*, watch the Discovery Channel or visit a museum without the constant drumbeat of millions and billions of years.

In a *Newsweek* article, "Science finds God," the author states:

"In 1905, John William Strutt determines the age of a rock: 2 billion years old, officially disproving James Ussher's 1650 assertion that, according to Genesis, the universe was created on Oct. 22, 4004 B.C." [112]

James Ussher is known for dating the age of the earth from a strictly biblical perspective. Was a young earth officially disproved? Is John William Strutt the official spokesman for mankind? Because he said these things, does it make it so?

---

112 Begley, Sharon/ Westley, Marian. Newsweek, Volume 132, Issue 3 July 20, 1998. Science Finds God.

Chapter Eleven

Dating the Rocks: Radiometric Dating

There are approximately forty techniques used to date the age of igneous rocks which were once part of lava flow. Igneous rocks contain radioactive elements that decay from one element to another. The primary/mother element decays to a second/ daughter element. The most well-known of these is uranium, which decays to lead. For example:

Radioactive Parent	Stable Daughter	Half life
Potassium 40	Argon 40	1.25 billion yrs.
Rubidium 87	Strontium 87	48.8 billion yrs.
Thorium 232	Lead 208	14 billion yrs.
Uranium 235	Lead 207	700 million yrs.
Uranium 238	Lead 206	4.5 billion yrs.
Carbon 14	Nitrogen 14	5730 yrs.

Dating radioactive materials is a highly technical process and involves subjective interpretation of data. Radioactive dating techniques are subject to the same suppositions that plague all evolutionary ideas and directly influence interpretation.

Furthermore, there are inherent problems in radioactive dating techniques such as the constant rate of decay, the preexistence of daughter elements and the resolution of anomalies.

The Rate of Decay

California's *Life Science* textbook states: "The rate of decay of each radioactive element is constant; it never changes."[113] This statement is an assumption that cannot be proven. Radiometric dating was discovered in 1905, so it is impossible to confirm any constant decay rate before then. All we can be certain of is that it appears to have been constant for about the last hundred years. Carbon 14, which science claims has a half-life of 5,730 years, would require another 5,730 years to conclusively prove its decay rate is constant.

Accelerated Decay

If the rate of nuclear decay has changed significantly at some point in the past, then any data based on radioactive decay would become meaningless. This rate change could have been during the creation of the earth itself, or perhaps Noah's flood, but it is conceivable that the rate of decay changes under extreme conditions. Other problems center around what is found that should not be here, and things that are found that are here. For example, there is a lack of Helium in the air, and too much Helium in the Rocks.

The RATE project was an eight-year study of radioisotopes and the age of the earth, sponsored by several creationist groups. This project sought to examine the fundamental assumptions of radiometric dating techniques. The details of this study are available in both technical writings as well as the popular book,

---

113 California Life Science. Prentice Hall, Boston Massachusetts. Upper Saddle River, New Jersey. 2008. pg. 280

Thousands Not Billions. According to the scientists involved in the RATE project:

> *If radioactive decay has been going on for millions and billions of years ... there is insufficient Helium in the air, and too much Helium in rocks. Recent experiments commissioned by the RATE group indicate that "1.5 billion years" worth of nuclear decay have taken place, but in one or more short periods 4000 - 8000 years ago. This would shrink the alleged 4.5-billion-year radioisotope age of the earth to only a few thousand years.*

> *Los Alamos measurements of uranium, thorium, and lead showed "1.5 billion" years' worth of nuclear decay at today's rates. After calculating how much helium had been deposited by decay, they then measured how much helium was still in the zircons. It turned out that up to 58% of the helium had not diffused out of the zircons; the percentages decreased with depth and temperature. At the time that the RATE group began its work, the diffusion rates had not been measured for the zircons and biotite. Based on the helium found in zircons, Dr. Russell Humphreys calculated the diffusion rates for both the Creation and the Uniformitarian models. He found that the diffusion rates for the two models differ by a factor of 100,000.*

> *When the diffusion rates in zircons were measured, they matched the Creation model but were found to be totally incompatible with the Uniformitarian model. These results, along with the helium observed in zircons, show that diffusion has been occurring for 6000 ± 2000 years. These rates are about 250,000 times too high for the Uni-*

Bridging the Origins Divide

formitarian model. This demonstrates that the observed decay of uranium cannot have taken 1.5 billion years.

For zircons to retain the observed amount of helium for 1.5 billion years, they would have had to have been at the temperature of liquid nitrogen (-196ºC below zero) for all that time, which is, of course, both incompatible with life and with any known or conjectured history of the earth.[114]

Presently the science concerning accelerated decay is incomplete, but so too is the big bang theory, and most scientific hypotheses concerning the creation of the earth. The point here is that science cannot be certain of what happened. The theories involved are based on naturalism and require subjective interpretation of the data. We do not know for certain if the decay rate is constant; however, there is good evidence that it is not. (Interestingly, the data has since been refined and updated to give a date of 5680 (+/- 2000) years.) [115]

Pre-existing Conditions

The presence of daughter isotopes in a rock immediately upon its formation would undermine the validity of any tests performed. In every case, the amount of daughter element pre-existing in each sample is unknown. Dr. John Morris wrote, If some daughter material is present at the start, the rock would appear to be old, when in fact it had just been formed.[116]

In recent lava flows, when we know the approximate age of a rock sample, the test should read zero. If the dating process is

---

114 creationwiki.org/Accelerated_decay
115 www.answersingenesis.org/
116 Morris, John. The Young Earth; Master Books, P.O. Box 727, Green Forest, AR 72638. pg. 54

accurate, then the date derived should be almost equivalent to zero, or too young to be measured. In the scientific literature, research results have been reported where rocks of known age have been dated. In almost every case the "age" of these recent lavas has come back from the lab in terms of excessively high ages, not essentially zero as one would predict.[117]

For example, the Sunset Crater flow in northern Arizona contains native Indian artifacts and it can be verified that the flow occurred nine hundred to one thousand years ago. Yet the radioactive ages given ranged from 210,000 and 230,000 years.

A three-hundred-year-old lava flow was dated at 485,000 years of age in Mt. Rangitoto in New Zealand. On Vulcan's throne in the Grand Canyon, a flow spoken of in Indian legends yielded a date of 117 million years.

A Closed System

There is no proof that the system is closed—the system being the possibility of movement between the various atoms and molecules in the rocks. In other words, we don't know if there has been any contamination or change in the chemical because they were corrupted by outside influences.

The Geologic Column

The geologic column is a tremendous blanket of sedimentary rock that has been found to cover the entire earth. Layers of flood, liberated deposits of sandstone, limestone and shale completely cover every landmass by hundreds of feet deep.

This thick stratum has been interpreted by scientists to represent 600 million years of life on earth. Aside from occasional areas of erosion and uplift, every square inch on earth is cov-

---

117 IBID pg. 54

     Bridging the Origins Divide

ered.[118] The chart below is a simplified representation of how the column is divided across time.

	Cenozoic—65 mya-present
Phanerozoic	Mesozoic—250-144 mya
	Paleozoic—600-286 mya
Precambrian	Proterozoic—2500 mya
	Archaean—3800 mya
	Hadean—4600 mya
mya = millions of years	

Radiometric dating did not exist when these ages for the column were contrived. The dates were arbitrarily assigned based on the assumption of slow gradual geological processes. Once the dates were set, they became the basis for estimating the ages of the rocks and fossils which are found in the various strata.

"Before radiometric dating was devised, uniformitarian geologists postulated periods of millions of years duration to slowly deposit the strata systems. A single sedimentary lamina, or bed, was supposed by uniformitarian geologists to represent typically a year or many years duration. It was concluded, therefore, that multiplied thousands of laminae and beds superimposed required millions of years.

"Recently, however, geologists have discovered that laminae and beds form quickly on floodplains of rivers during floods, in shallow marine areas during storms, and in deep water by turbidity currents. The evidence of rapid sedimentation is now so easily recognized that geologists observing a strata system these days often ask where to

---

118 nwcreation.net/geologycolumn.html accessed October 1, 2024

*insert the missing time of which the strata do not show
sedimentary evidence.*

*Catastrophism, quite naturally, is making a comeback.
There is good reason to believe that entire strata systems, and even groups of systems, were accumulated in
a hydraulic cataclysm matching the description of Noah's
Flood in the Bible."*[119]

Circular Reasoning

Mesozoic rocks and fossils are believed to be 250 to 144 million
years old. The only method available for dating fossils is Carbon 14, but it is unreliable beyond 50,000 to 100,000 years. A
fossil's age is determined by its assigned place in the geological
column. It cannot be independently verified.

The ages of rocks are also determined by their place in the
column. Samples which can be tested are subjected to a variety
of radioactive tests until one is found that fits the assumptive
age of the specimen.[120] If a test result indicates an age outside its
parameters, it is considered contaminated and disallowed. In
essence, the rocks date the fossils and the fossils date the rocks.

Most of the Grand Canyon is composed of fossil-bearing
sedimentary layers which cannot be dated with radiometric
techniques. However, there are two layers which can be dated.

The first is the Cardenas Basalts, which are thought to be
the oldest of all canyon rocks. They have been dated between
715 million to 1.07 billion years of age, a difference of almost
300 million years.[121]

---

119 Ten Misconceptions about the Geologic Column, By Steven A. Austin, PhD
120 IBID
121 Morris, John. The Young Earth; Master Books, P.O. Box 727, Green Forest, AR 72638.
      pg. 58, 59

                        Bridging the Origins Divide

The second layer follows the canyon rim and is considered the youngest of all rocks at around a few thousand years. These lava flows may have been witnessed by native Americans. However, the dates given by many different techniques begin at 3.6 million and go to 117 million, then to 1.34 billion with the highest age at 2.6 billion years of age.[122]

Are obtained dates accurate?

Dr. Morris asks, *"When does the method work, and on what basis can one determine which specimens are valid just by looking at the field evidence?"*[123]

In other words, which rocks do we choose? If older rocks are brought to the surface and intermingled with new rock, how does that work? Does science appreciate every possible cause of contamination? Do they know the history of each sample they test? Can we ever be certain their findings are accurate?

The only way to know if a prescribed date is accurate is if it fits within the expected outcome. If that criterion is met, the test is considered valid. A truly scientific process should be consistent, not just when it supports a presupposition.

The Kapalua lava flow has had many anomalous dates using various methods. The 1800–1801 AD eruption is too young to have produced argon or helium; yet large quantities have been found. The flow has been dated from between 4–140 million years to 2.96 billion years.[124]

The explanation for the discrepancy in the above ages was that very old magma must have come up from the earth's core and mixed with younger rocks. To accurately date a rock, you must

---

122 IBID
123 IBID pg 55
124 IBID pg 55

know the specific history of the sample being tested, which is impossible to determine. Dr. Morris writes,

> *"With rocks of a known age, such as the Hualapai flow, the radioisotope dating doesn't work. When there are rocks of an unknown age, radioisotope dating is assumed to work."*[125]

These dating techniques are flawed from the outset. Comparative studies by their very nature must have an objective starting point, a standard to measure from. The investigator must understand all possible factors that could influence the outcome.

If one were to study calcium loss in women between the ages of 12 and 82 but only tested the 82-year-old women, it would not be scientific. This is what we are being asked to believe when it comes to the dating of igneous rocks. Scientists are basing their entire philosophy of life on defending and maintaining an old age concept of the universe.

Mount St. Helens

On May 18, 1980, Mount St. Helens erupted. In a single day, large canyons were formed, thousands of trees and animals were destroyed and 57 people died. Imagine what would have happened if there were many such eruptions during the Flood. If these current entities were combined with those of the flood waters described in the Bible, the geological "changes" would be unimaginable.[126]

According to Dr. Jason Lisle of the Bible Science Institute in Colorado Springs, Colorado, studies of lava flow from the Mount St. Helens volcano have revealed that rocks tested for

---

125 IBID pg. 56
126 There is much to learn from this eruption, I would encourage the reader to watch "Is Genesis History" on YouTube.

 Bridging the Origins Divide

radiometric dating were over a million years of age. This was from a known and dated lava flow, demonstrating that radiometric testing is not accurate or trustworthy.[127]

Additional testing has been conducted on rocks of a known age from lava flows in Hawaii. They have consistently been shown to be millions of years old.

Dr. Lisle asks how one can trust in the dating of rocks of an unknown age when testing rocks of a known age are off by millions of years.[128]

The Fossil Record

Long thought to represent the evolutionary development of life on earth, the fossil record is more likely the order of death during a flood of such magnitude. The least mobile and unintelligent would die first (hard shelled sea creatures). Beings with more intelligence and mobility would survive longer and escape the initial consequences of the flood. Mammals would have perished before humans, who would have been the last to die. Consider which fossils are in the geological column:

95% of all fossils are marine invertebrates, particularly shellfish. Of the remainder, 4.75% are algae and plant fossils. 95% of the remaining 0.25% consists of the other invertebrates, including insects (.2375%). The remaining 0.0125% includes all vertebrates, mostly fish. [...] Only about 1,200 dinosaur skeletons have been found. 95% of the mammal fossils were deposited during the Ice Age.[129]

One of the greatest ironies of modern science is the sugges-

127 www.youtube.com/watch?v=pR7P_6OOJCw
128 www.youtube.com/watch?v=_SNJveKld5I biblicalscienceinstitute.com/origins/
    creation-101-radiometric-dating-and-the-age-of-the-earth
129 Morris, John. The Young Earth; Master Books, P.O. Box 727, Green Forest, AR 72638.
    pg. 70

tion that the planet Mars was destroyed by a massive flood.[130] Presently, Mars is an arid desert without any known water on its surface. If you suggest to most modern scientists that the earth was flooded by a global flood, they will laugh in your face. Yet 75% of the earth's surface is covered with water almost two miles deep.

> *"They deliberately forget that long ago by God's word the heavens existed, and the earth was formed out of water and by water, and the world of that time was deluged and destroyed."*
>
> —2 Peter 3:5

The Formation of Fossils

California's Life Science textbook tells us how they believe fossils are formed.

> *First, an ancient crocodile dies and sinks to the bottom of a river. Layers of sediments cover the crocodile's body. Over millions of years the sediments harden to become rock, the crocodile is preserved as a fossil. The rock erodes. The fossil is exposed on the surface of a rock.[131]*

The formations of fossils are one key in understanding earth's history, much of evolution's theory is based on their understanding of the fossil record. It is difficult to understand how any scientist can believe that fossils are formed as they have suggested. It requires blind faith to accept their definition as true.

> *Any mammal which dies in water will initially bloat and rise to the surface. Decomposition begins immediately.*

---

130 news.harvard.edu/gazette/story/2022/01/mars-surface-shaped-by-catastrophic-flooding
131 California Life Science. Prentice Hall, 2008. Pg. 285

They will dismember, disintegrate, or be quickly scavenged in a watery environment. Flood waters quickly destroy soft-bodied organisms and preserve those with hard outer shells. Unless the organism is completely and quickly covered, it will not survive as a fossil.

Today fossilization is a rare event and is simply not expected to occur on a global scale. Decomposition is the rule following death, unless the matter is buried rapidly and to a depth that would prevent microbial digestion and oxidation. Hard shelled animals that burrow into sediment are expected to be fossilized, along with large and heavy bones through chance circumstances. However, every kind of animal alive today is found in the fossil record. Many are completely intact, and some specimens show literally no signs of decomposition.

To become fossilized, a plant or animal must usually have hard parts, such as bone, or wood. It must be buried quickly to prevent decay and must be undisturbed throughout the long process.

The data concerning fossils of the earth more readily represents a global flood. Deceased life forms would not fossilize slowly over millions of years; they would decay rapidly.

Christians often say it doesn't matter if Genesis 1 and 2 are interpreted as a six-day creation as long we believe God is the creator. I believe one can be a faithful believer and still accept evolution and millions of years of creation for the heavens and the earth if one recognizes God as Creator.

Conversely, I firmly believe that rejection of the Genesis record and allegiance to evolutionary beliefs undermines the Christian faith. It begins with Bible interpretation and the unintended consequences of what defines a day. The most obvious interpretation of the Genesis record is that God created the heavens and earth in six solar days. While there are minor difficulties with this interpretation, it is very sound exegetically. It avoids changing the meaning of "day" and reading long ages of time into the text, which undermine the authority of the Scriptures and does not satisfy the claims of science.

As believers, everything we trust begins with the existence of an eternal, all-powerful Creator. This belief is the foundation of reality and the faith. We know God exists because creation demonstrates this.

> *"For the wrath of God is revealed from heaven against all ungodliness and unrighteousness of men, who by their unrighteousness suppress the truth, what can be known about God is plain to them, because God has shown it to them. For his invisible attributes, namely, his eternal power and divine nature, have been clearly perceived, ever since the creation of the world, in the things that have been made. So, they are without excuse. For although they knew God, they did not honor him as God or give thanks to him, but they became futile in their thinking, and their foolish hearts were darkened. Claiming to be wise, they became fools and exchanged the glory of the immortal God for images resembling mortal man and birds and animals and creeping things."*

> —Romans 1:19-23

Natural revelation shows us that God exists. He is all-powerful, all knowing, good and just. His justice demands He must com-

Bridging the Origins Divide

municate to those he will eventually judge. God could not be just without clearly giving us rules we must follow as the basis for his judgment. As Christians we believe the Scriptures are God's means of communication to humanity and that they are true and accurate in all they say. It is an objective basis for faith. Undermining them undermines the faith.

Appendix One:

Talking Points

Section 1: Is There a Creator?
Belief in a Creator is a self-evident truth and understood through reason, not blind faith or religious indoctrination.

Belief in a Creator is a philosophical question for which science has no answer. Investigation into the existence of a Creator must begin with an open mind and proper suppositions and not upon the bias of naturalism.

Nothingness cannot produce something; therefore, someone or something has always existed.

That which has always existed must have had a cause. Since structured, designed matter and complex life forms exist, they must have been caused.

The universe and life forms are far too complex to have been created by random chance.

Natural selection and the big bang are possible processes, not causes. Therefore, by themselves they could not create the universe or simple or complex life forms. They would be dependent on someone or another power as their source.

Human beings are of infinite value. If matter or natural selection were the creator, nothing would matter at all. Human beings and all life forms as we know them would be animated dust without purpose.

Human decisions have eternal consequences. If matter or natural selection were the creator, there would be no basis for morality. Every action would be equally valid. Murder and rape would be as valuable as love and protection. What we do would be utterly insignificant and without meaning.

Section 2: What is the Creator Like?

Since it is necessary for something to always exist, the Creator must be an eternal being.

Since it required great power and intelligence to create the universe and all life forms, the Creator must be powerful and intelligent.

Since it is illogical for evil to be the source of a benevolent universe and loving relationships, it is logical that the Creator is good.

Since it is necessary for life to have a source of meaning and morality, the Creator must also be the final arbiter for all human actions. He must be just.

Since mankind's choices have serious consequences, a good creator is obligated to communicate his expectations to us so that he will be just in his judgment of our actions.

Section 3: Is the Creator the God of the Bible?

The discerned characteristics of the Creator are in complete agreement with the God of the Bible.

Science claims to have proven that the Bible is not accurate in its account of the creation of the universe and all life forms.

The best interpretation of the biblical record is that it places the universe at between 6 and 10 thousand years old. Science believes it is billions of years old.

Scientific evidence is based on unproven and unprovable assumptions such as,

- naturalism—no supernatural involvement in the creation of the universe.
- uniformity—all natural processes presently observed have always been this way.
- the manner in which the Creator made the universe.
- the assumed ages of the geologic column.
- a constant rate of radioactive decay.
- the known amount of daughter elements present before radiometric dating is attempted.
- a flawed understanding of the fossilization process.

The concepts of naturalism, uniformity, long geological ages and a rejection of the Great Flood were prophesied in the book of Peter in the New Testament.

Evolution is a direct fulfillment of these prophecies, and it should give us pause to accept that theory considering the clear teachings of the Bible.

The documentary hypothesis teaches that the Old Testament Scriptures were written several centuries later than Jewish and Christian scholars had believed. The view throughout history was that Moses wrote the Torah between 1500 and 1300 BC using a variety of original sources.

Julius Wellhausen speculated that Judaism was originally polytheistic and eventually evolved into a monotheistic religion well after the time of Moses. This theory is based in part on four primary assumptions:

Evolution is true in religion as well as the natural world.

There was no written language at the time of Moses. The discovery of the Elba tablets completely disproved this theory.

All supernatural events in the Bible were mythological and untrue.

The usage of different names for God used in various sections of the Torah meant there were different authors.

All "scholarship" associated with the documentary hypothesis has been refuted and answered by conservative scholarship. There is no reason to believe any of the opinions it holds are historically accurate. There is no reason to doubt the conservative date for the writing of the Scripture.

Josh McDowell's *The New Evidence That Demands a Verdict* has an extensive discussion on this topic. (See part 3, section II, pp 389-412.)

Appendix Two:

Is the Bible a Myth?

It is worth noting that some consider the biblical account of creation mythological. *Live Science* lists the Genesis record as the number one mythological account of creation. However, when you consider the biblical account alongside truly mythological accounts, there is no comparison.

The mother of the Aztec creation story was Coatlicue (Lady of the Skirt of Snakes). She was created in the image of the unknown, decorated with skulls, snakes and lacerated hands. There are no cracks in her body, and she is a perfect monolith. She is a sum total of intensity and self-containment, yet her features are square.

Coatlicue was first impregnated by an obsidian knife and gave birth to Coyolxauhqui (goddess of the moon) and to a group of male offspring who became the night stars. Coatlicue once found a ball of feathers, which she tucked into her bosom. Later, she realized it was gone, at which time she realized she was again pregnant. Her children (the moon and stars) did not believe her story. Ashamed of their mother, they resolved to kill her. A goddess could only give birth once to the original litter of divinity and no more.

While the children plotted her demise, Coatlicue gave birth to the fiery god of war, Huitzilopochtli. With the help of a fire serpent, he destroyed his brothers and sister. He beheaded Coyolxauhqui and threw her body into a deep mountain gorge, where it lies dismembered forever.

The natural cosmos of the Indians was born of catastrophe; the heavens literally crumbled to pieces. The earth mother fell and was fertilized. Her children were torn apart by fratricide, disjointed and scattered throughout the universe.

The Bible's account has God creating the universe in six days and creating Eve from Adam's rib. No aspect of the biblical record is remotely like the Aztec or other mythological creation story.

The existence of an eternal, all-powerful creator challenges the assumptions of naturalism and anti-supernaturalism; however, it does not make the Bible's record mythological. An all-powerful supernatural being can intervene in the natural order any time he wishes, without nullifying the natural order of the universe.

Science has never fully explained the cause of the big bang or the process of natural selection. Since it is impossible for a complex ordered universe to exist apart from a supernatural creator, the biblical account remains the only rational, non-mythological, non-scientific explanation for this universe.

Appendix Three:

The Problem of Religion

Evidence for this is found in the writings and statements of prominent atheists who often appeal to the history of religion as an argument against the existence of a creator. They appear to reject the Creator because of the actions of those who claim to know Him.

Sam Harris said, "It is terrible that we all die and lose everything we love; it is doubly terrible that so many human beings suffer needlessly while alive. That so much of this suffering can be directly attributed to religion—to religious hatreds, religious wars, religious delusions and religious diversions of scarce resources—is what makes atheism a moral and intellectual necessity."

Richard Dawkins said, "My last vestige of hands-off-religion respect disappeared in the smoke and choking dust of September 11th, 2001, followed by the National Day of Prayer, when prelates and pastors did their tremulous Martin Luther King impersonations and urged people of mutually incompatible faiths to hold hands, united in homage to the very force that caused the problem in the first place."

There is no justification for many things that have been done in the name of religion over the centuries. There is a need to answer the charges against religion, many of which are obviously true. I find myself in agreement and personally reject the ideas and beliefs of many religious institutions. However, many scientists, philosophers, kings and presidents have done evil in the name of their office or discipline.

The question is not, *Have human beings done atrocious and unacceptable things in the name of God?* The question is, *Is there a God to do these things in their name?* Just because I say I am doing something in God's name does not mean I am.

Appendix Four:

Anti-Supernaturalism

Naturalism's influence is evident in other areas of study. Most modern Bible scholars reject miracles on the same basis as Dawkins and other scientists.

The parting of the Red Sea is one such example. The Bible text clearly teaches that God supernaturally parted the Red Sea so the Israelites could safely cross over on dry land with a wall of water on both sides. When the Egyptians followed, God allowed the water to return, killing them all.

The exact location of this crossing is unknown, though it could have been the Gulf of Aqua bah. The Hebrew word *sup* is translated in different ways. The English version of the text is defined as "red sea." In 1 Kings 9:26, *sup* refers to the Gulf of Aqua bah.

Under the influence of naturalism, theologians have maintained that the interpretation is not "red sea," but "sea of reeds"—a shallow marshland. If a strong wind had formed and dried out the land where the Israelites crossed, how then could the entire Egyptian army drown in a foot of water? Interestingly, a *History Channel* special shows how the Israelites ambushed and killed the Egyptians in the Sea of Reeds.

Did the Israelites cross the Red Sea because God separated the waters, or did the entire Egyptian army drown in a naturally formed foot of water? Neither would be feasible if one did not believe in miracles. If you believe miracles are possible, then go with what is written.

Appendix Five:

Starlight and Time

I have not attempted to answer the question of the speed of light. One of the arguments for the age of the earth is the distance of the farthest star from the Earth. If light travels at 186,282,397 miles per second, it would take approximately 13.79 billion years for the light to reach the earth. Hence, the universe would be 13.79 billion years old.

The solution to this problem from a young earth perspective has been sought for decades. At this time there are many theories, none of which seem to solve all the issues surrounding this question.

I must say that even though we may not have an exact answer to this question, it does not shake my belief in a young earth or a six-day creation.

I would encourage the reader to go biblicalscienceinstitute. com and read a series of articles written by Dr. Jason Lisle. Click the Topics link on the dashboard and click on Astronomy, scroll to Distant Starlight, and read the articles within that link. Dr.

Lisle has given an excellent overview of the various theories and has given a compelling solution to this difficult issue.

In my opinion, Dr. Lisle is one of the most intelligent and thorough astrophysicists/scientists in the world. He is a prolific writer, and any book he has written is highly recommended.

If you have questions concerning the concepts I have written about; the age of the Earth, radiometric dating, etc., his books will give you a deeper scientific explanation.